POST-TRAUMATIC STRESS REVELATIONS

Afrah Caraballo

SEVEN KEY REVELATIONS FOR REINTEGRATING YOUR POST-TRAUMATIC WARRIOR

POST-TRAUMATIC STRESS REVELATIONS
SEVEN KEY REVELATIONS FOR REINTEGRATING YOUR POST-TRAUMATIC WARRIOR

Book Editor: Callysta Caraballo
Photo Editor: Antonio Rios III

iUniverse books may be ordered through booksellers or by contacting:

iUniverse
1663 Liberty Drive
Bloomington, IN 47403
www.iuniverse.com
1-800-Authors (1-800-288-4677)

ISBN: 978-1-5320-4972-9 (sc)
ISBN: 978-1-5320-4971-2 (hc)
ISBN: 978-1-5320-4970-5 (e)

Library of Congress Control Number: 2018905887

Print information available on the last page.

iUniverse rev. date: 06/25/2018

CONTENTS

ACKNOWLEDGEMENTS

Thank you to my creator for your love and every presence. To all of the angels and guides who are perfectly placed to facilitate my growth; thank you. To my greatest teachers Callysta and Kaynen, my compass and anchor; because of you, I have my heading. Thank you to my Emah Yahkeemah, (Paula Comer-White), the rich and generous soil that nurtured me when I was just a young and tender sprout; your love and light has fueled my journey in countless ways. You are such a big part of the woman I have become; todah!

Thank you to all of the amazing trauma survivors and caregivers who work so bravely and tirelessly on the healing path. To the warriors in and out of uniform who find the wisdom and courage to heal, and be healed, I am inspired and encouraged by you daily. I am honored to work with and for you.

INTRODUCTION

The beauty, and tragedy, of our adaptability is how trauma survivors can either get stuck on an emotional roller-coaster of judgement, guilt and shame, or get off, heal, and grow into something better and new. Without judgment, guilt and shame, the possibilities are endless. The pile of crap left behind following a traumatic event can either become your life or the fertilizer you use to grow a new life. There is no 'getting back to normal.' Posttraumatic means after a traumatic event. A traumatic event is anything that causes you to feel terrified, horrified, helpless and hopeless. It is anything that shatters *your* sense of safety and wholeness in the world. Once this has occurred you are completely and forever changed. So, there is no going back to 'normal.' At the point of post trauma—after trauma, you have two choices; move forward or stay stuck. This book is an attempt to help survivors get off the emotional roller-coaster of judgment, guilt and shame, and start moving toward the healing life of their choice. How fast you move is not important; just move. In the words of Martin Luther King Jr.: I invite you to move forward—crawl if you cannot walk; walk if you cannot run; run if you cannot fly, or fly toward your next best Self. What's important is that you move, and keep moving toward your next best Self.

Because trauma is about a complete loss of control, over yourself and your environment, the posttraumatic life becomes a series of extreme choices that are attempts to regain control and prevent that traumatic event from ever happening again.

Trauma is a terrifying, horrifying surprise that leaves you feeling helpless and hopeless. Your age, circumstances or life experience can all affect if, and when, you are traumatized. Trauma is about loss. It's an equal opportunity offender, and we all lose something important at some point in our lives. But the response and support, or lack thereof, that follow a traumatic event will have enormous implications on the posttraumatic life. Without the appropriate support, a trauma survivor's life becomes about *never* getting caught off guard again. The extreme choices designed to cope with the loss become labels like: control freak, alcoholic, workaholic, drug addict, depressed, anxious, defiant, angry, oppositional, withdrawn, isolated, bipolar, borderline personality, schizophrenic, lazy, bitch, asshole, doormat, slut, antisocial, and on and on. Often, it's much easier to label, and be labelled, than it is to hear, witness or share the traumatic event/s that lead to these behaviors. The judgment, guilt and shame attached to each, and every, label are barriers to healing; these barriers prevent you from freely driving your own vehicle and living your own life. Judgment, guilt and shame have a way of keeping you "in your place." As you consider what this means, think about these question:

What place?

Whose place?

Who assigned this place?

Who benefits from you staying in "your place"?

How does it benefit you?

What does it cost you?

I invite you to look at these questions closely, and I would be willing to bet that the answers are held by a trauma survivor/offender with a vested interest in your staying stuck 'in your place.' Being stuck is a coping skill, however maladaptive—it is a way of trying to stay 'safe.' In this stuck place, there is the safety of knowing what to expect, never mind how horrible or painful—at least there are no surprises. But this is the thinking of a traumatized person (a wounded person). "At least I know what to expect," victims will say. And in doing so, we can stay stuck in the cycle of judgment, guilt and shame—the prison of the trauma victim. In this way, we become the warden and the prisoner. You are invited now to entertain the idea of freedom. Freedom from pain, freedom from fear, and freedom from loneliness are all available to us. But freedom is not free; it costs time, effort, courage, trust, faith and hope. These can seem too high a price for those of us locked in the prison of judgment, guilt and shame.

A trauma bond is a very powerful thing and can be nearly impossible to break out of. It is the cement that holds together the walls of the prison that stand between you and the next best version of you. There's an official term for this bond, "Stockholm syndrome." This phenomenon occurs when the trauma survivor/victim becomes bonded, emotionally and psychologically, to the offender and feels compelled to protect and/or defend her, him or them, depending on the situation. In any case, the victim is misguided into believing that the offender is also the rescuer or (in some cases) the victim. When the offense is ongoing, the victim is isolated and the offender(s) become the sole source if emotional and physical supply, distorting the messages of love and support. This distortion damages the victim's ability to make healthy choices about their own wellbeing. When food, shelter, safety and belonging (all primal needs) are withheld and manipulated by the offender, the victim becomes dependent on the offender for life sustaining resources. In this way, the relationship is more like a triangular trap where victim and offender interchange the roles of victim, offender and rescuer. This trauma trap, or trauma bond, is preserved by the beliefs motivated by judgement, guilt, and shame. The offender(s) will say things like, 'you made me do this to you,' 'you know I can't help myself,' 'I need you' (victim stance); or they'll apologize and nurture the victim, providing food, comforts or gifts, after the offense, making promises to behave better in the future (rescuer stance); then offend again.

This triangulation is not exclusive to civilian life. We make the mistake of trying to simplify the word trauma. We want a neat definition. We want a neat package to label **trauma**. Well, there is no neat word for the disgusting, life shattering surprising event(s) that traumatizes a person. Medically, trauma means wound or injury; would means a breach in the integrity of the skin, which can range from a scrape to a severed limb. Psychologically, trauma means the same thing, except there is no x-ray for a bruised or shattered heart, mind or spirit. Because we cannot see the damage, we are forced to judge based on the behaviors of trauma victims. So, judge with compassion. Trauma is an equal opportunity offender. It doesn't care about your age, race, gender, economic status, physical or intellectual abilities. Anyone, anywhere, can lose something important, and be at risk of feeling helpless, hopeless, horrified and terrified— anyone. If you are human, you have something, or someone, that you cannot imagine life without; something that makes life worth living for you. This can be a house, a car, a job, a professional title, a pet, a friend, a family member, a comrade, battle buddy, fellow service member, anything or anyone you hold dear can be lost or threatened. We are both vulnerable and resilient; meaning we can be wounded physically, mentally and emotionally AND we CAN HEAL. That we are interdependent can be scary, or off putting, especially when trauma occurs at the hands of a human offender. Natural disasters are typically easier to recover from than are human-to-human violations. That we are physiologically designed to interrelate can also be encouraging; because as long as we're alive, there is something or someone to live for. What happened to you, is not who you are. What you have survived has changed you, but it did not kill you.

Unfortunately, after the physical trauma ends, victims can

become stuck repeating these scenarios internally or in other relationships. Getting stuck in the moment of loss, can imprison us. Often victims blame themselves for the loss, or offense, and create a cycle of self-induced abuse and neglect. Staying bonded to the traumatic event, or the offender, keeps survivors from growing into the next best version of themselves. The revelations intended here, are that no one <u>has</u> to stay stuck in the pile of crap. No one *has to* carry the hemorrhaging wound of loss indefinitely. Freedom from the pain, and horror, of trauma is available to anyone; regardless of what you've been told. Regardless of what you've done, or what's been done to you. The trauma bond is strong AND you are stronger. You can heal. You can rebuild. You can grow into something better.

Some of the most fertile soil, is the result of what we have defined as vile waste and/or catastrophe—volcanic soil or horse manure, for example, produce some of the most beautiful and delicious food and vegetation on our planet. And I'm sure you've heard countless stories of beautiful and successful people who rose from unspeakable horrors to become the celebrities we see now. We celebrate these transformations in life and nature; yet we act as if the same transformations are somehow beyond us, or unavailable to us. I invite you to see with new eyes the possibility that you are made of the same essence as a volcano, a pile of manure, a forest fire, slavery, holocaust, apartheid—Harriet Tubman, Victor Frankel, Nelson Mandela, Gandhi, Martin Luther King Jr. or Oprah Winfrey. Even when suppressed or oppressed, living beings can survive and grow. Nelson Mandela is quoted as saying "It always seems impossible until it's done." You don't have to look very far to recognize strength, courage and possibility in others—a friend, a family member, a neighbor, a coworker or a church member. Every day people doing the seemingly impossible, are all around us. Every living being has within them the ability to grow and thrive, when allowed and supported.

Every choice you make is calculated. Do…? Or Don't do…? Maybe, is simply a delayed do, or don't do. Indecision, is a decision! It is the decision to let something, or someone make the decision for you. So, unless you're physically unconscious, you are calculating every choice you make. Go to the restroom now, or wait? Like most decisions, it's only a matter of time before you go. The conditions under which you choose to go are up to you. I remember being in Air Force basic training where my TI (training instructor) yelled his expectations at us about the six weeks that would follow. He commanded, "do not ask me to go to the bathroom! If I say no, you will eventually disobey me!" Nearly twenty years later, and I can still hear his voice vividly. Of all the commands he could give us, and with as much control as he had over us, at the end of the day, we still had control over our choices. The choice to stay or go, and under what conditions, was always ours. Even in situations that are not voluntary such as prison, war, rape, robbery, earthquake, forest fire, hurricane or any other horrible or unpleasant circumstance, you choose how you think, feel and behave in response. In all situations, you calculate in favor of life for yourself or someone/something you love. If I do…I'll live. If I do…I'll live longer than if I do…that. If I do…I may die but, my family, my friend, my country, or my beliefs and values will survive. So, that in the end, what's most important to us, is relationship. And we make choices based on the value we place on the relationships in our lives. We are constantly in relationship; with ourselves, and our environment. There's no getting around it. If you are alive, you are in relationship with something or someone: your dog, cat, horse, family member, friend, house, job car or addiction. The greater the perceived value of the relationships, the more time and energy you are willing to spend maintaining them, or the more you are willing to risk protecting them.

Sometime, the relationship is with the traumatized part of yourself (your warrior self). I will discuss this in more detail later. But this part of you is the part that takes over when the loving and trusting part of you is betrayed, when the caring part of you feels neglected and alone; this warrior version of you only wants to keep you *'safe.'* For me, this warrior was awakened when I was six years old and was sent to live with various strangers for a total of four years. I was born in Israel to a rebel couple with dreams of peace, hope, love and freedom. My parents were born in Chicago in the 1940s (not the best time in history for Black people in the U.S.), to parents who migrated north from the deep south. Even with the political climate of the time, they managed to get a good education, go to college and had opportunities that many Blacks didn't in those days. But they were still Black in America during the 50s, 60s, and 70's. I can only imagine the kind of unspeakable acts of discrimination, and segregation, they endured during that time. My aunts and uncles would tell me stories about how difficult life was for them, and the drastic differences in life 'up north' from 'down south,' when they would visit relatives in Tennessee and Mississippi. By the time my parents met each other, they had both had enough, and decided to join a religious group (a cult) that fed their need for a sense of safety, belonging, self-worth, respect, hope and peace. This group decided that 'The Promised Land' (Israel) was the place to find these things. So, not speaking the language, and with no idea how they would manage, they took the leap. This group's philosophy is based in the Old Testament of the Bible, so it was very conservative and rigid (especially for females). And as fate would have it, I was my father's first born (mixed blessing there, being female). The circumstances of my birth are a book all its own, but the short of it is, at birth, I was ADORED. For the first six years of my life, I KNEW I was loved, wanted and safe.

This all changed when I, along with all the other six and seven-year-old kids in the commune, was piled into a produce truck and shipped off to live with strangers, but who were also members of the cult. Suddenly, I'm living in a place without my parents and the people who had loved and nurtured me for my entire little life. I remember the moment my warrior woke up. I was six years old and standing at a sliding glass door looking out at an enclosed yard. I had been in the new city for about a week or so, when it dawned on me that I was stuck here. I was alone and had to make the best of it. So, I turned my attention to my peers. Many of whom were sad and afraid. I remember feeling concerned; but not scared; so, I would reassure them that it would be ok, and that it would all work out. It was during these two years that I was sexually molested for the first time, by a teenaged girl, and later an attempt by an adult male. Even this didn't shake my sense of self; I still believed this was all just a big mistake, and that my parents would come take me home. Well they didn't. Because of their background, they were instrumental in teaching and supporting the infrastructure of this new 'nation.' Looking back, in my own way, I guess I was attempting to do the same thing. So, two years passed, and now at the age of eight, we were all shipped to yet a different city, again to live with strangers, who were also members of the cult. This time things were worse. It was during these two years that physical and psychological abuse started. It was here that my warrior grew bigger and became angry! She became cunning, suspicious and withdrawn. There was still a sense of caring for my peers, but a complete distrust of adults began to grow. It was during this time that I realized that not only are my parents not coming for me, but that I was on my own. No one was to be trusted. Everyone was suspect. And at the end of the two years, in what I thought was the devil's playground, we were returned to our parents. Now I was ten years old and practically a handmaid to my younger siblings and my father's second wife. With four years of separation from my parents, there was a distance between us that would never be mended. My parents were different now. I was different now. The bond was broken; the cult had changed us as well as our priorities. Throughout our childhood, my peers and I were taught "your parent is any adult [in the cult] who does the will of God." What we didn't know to ask, was the 'will of God' according to whom? So back 'home,' with my parents, in my father's house, in the same city, but worlds apart, my plight continued. Realizing now that my previous calculations were correct—I am alone; I began to plan my escape. To where, I was not sure. Being a girl, I had not seen much, and I had not been taught anything about how to survive without a male present to make decisions for me. My warrior-self did not care! She would protect me from ever being betrayed, violated or abandoned again. This new 'reality' would get me through the next twenty plus years of my life. I started running. I ran away three times when I was fourteen years old, and the third time, I left and didn't look back for twenty-six years.

While I had no plan or direction, I knew I would never be at the mercy of anyone ever again. So, when my mother suggested coming to the U.S., I refused; citing all the reasons I had heard my entire life about why they left America, 'Babylon.' But, after months of running and struggling to survive, I started questioning and negotiating with her. Israel was my home, and while I didn't want to live in the commune anymore, I certainly did not want to leave home. My mother knew how important and education was, especially for a girl, so she stressed to me how a formal education could equip me with options no matter where I decided to live. I reluctantly agreed to go to America, get a high school diploma, and promptly return home. But this was not to be.

I arrived in the U.S. in 1987 and spent the next five years in Tennessee. What a rude awakening that was! With English as my second language, I had to learn to read and write in a 'backward' language (Hebrew is a right-to-left language) that breaks every rule it has. In addition, I had to learning how to be

'Black.' This may sound strange; but, until I came to the States, I was just a girl. I didn't become a 'Black Girl,' until I arrived in the United States; where I was repeatedly questioned about my behavior and informed that 'something's wrong with you.' "Why you talk like that!?" "Why you dress like that!?" "What's wrong with you!?" were common questions for the first 15 plus years of my life in this country; first in Memphis Tennessee and then in Chicago Illinois. I had never experienced racism until I move to the U.S, only sexism. Needless to say- but I will- culture shock, culture shock, culture shock! In 1987, I was surprised at the racial divide, and the rigidity, from both sides, to maintain it. I tell people, being in Israel, my problem was not having a penis, and being in America my problem became not being White. So, there I was, trying to learn how, and where, I fit in; with many confused, and well-meaning, people trying to 'put me in my place.' It was a very lonely time; I wasn't Black enough to be African-American, and not White. Being a teenager is hard enough; being a foreigner who looks like she's one thing but acts, talks and dresses like she's something else; you've got a recipe for trauma drama. And we all know how cruel insecure teenagers can be. Let's just say the welcoming committee dropped the ball on this one.

Until arriving to the States, I had been a strict Vegan. In the commune, nothing from an animal was permitted; no dairy, no meat and all meals were homemade. So, the discovery of processed foods and meat, made my first few years in America quite interesting. Fried chicken to start; then pizza! And the magic of sugary breakfast cereals! Fast and easy foods became my addiction/medication. I went from a size 8 to a size 18. In high school, math and choir were my refuge. I thrived in both. I earned a full-ride singing scholarship to college upon graduation. But, when I graduated at the age of nineteen, and got my first taste of freedom, I lost my mind. No one to tell me what to do, where to be, how to dress, what to eat, how to behave or question my choices. I was FREE! My warrior had had enough! She was on a mission of righteous justice! No more submissive girl, at the mercy of authoritative men (or women). I started smoking cigarettes, just because I could. And when I learned that my choir director was hurt that his first soprano was smoking, that just fueled the rebellious fire. I blew off the scholarship and decided I didn't need a college degree to tell me who I was. I floundered for about a year, which must have terrified my mother, because she called my older brother (the only man I would listen to at the time) to come and get me. He moved me to Chicago to reenroll in school and get me 'back on track.' But the warrior was having none of it! I turned 21, and all hell broke loose. I had a car, a decent paycheck and nothing but me to spend it on. That was a crazy five years! After five years of recklessness, I decided the Air Force was a good way to see the world, get back to Israel and maybe get back to college someday. But no, a year and a half in I learned that I had a brain tumor requiring medication and eventually surgery. I ended up being medically discharged. Now pregnant and 'disabled,' what am I going to do? The Air Force was the only 'conscious' career plan I had made.

I always knew I wanted and would have children. The brain tumor threatened to derail that but didn't. The birth of my daughter was my saving Grace. She changed me. She gave me a reason to live again. No more running. No more just surviving. I remember holding her in my arms at three weeks old, and looking into her deep, dark and beautiful eyes; lost in a love I had forgotten was possible, I was paralyzed. Looking back at me, I felt/heard, her say, "now what?" In that moment, I felt naked, transparent and unworthy; all at once. From that moment on, I was on a mission to prove myself worthy of this Angel. Until that point, I had been running. Running from what? I didn't know at the time. I now know that I was running from my past, from myself and from love, out of fear of being betrayed. Until that point, I didn't care who I hurt or how I was perceived by others. It was me against the world. But this little innocent and defenseless baby, called me out. Setting the stage for my next transformation. My new plan was to make something of myself; to prove myself worthy of this baby, this proof of unconditional love and trust. So, I thought share the love. I wanted to make sure all mothers felt what I was feeling. But how? How do I spread the message of love, hope and healing throughout the world? So, after several attempts at quick and easy, that didn't work out, I decided to get back in school. With a mission to be worthy and share the love. I started on a major in education (I would be a teacher), but the curriculum was too restrictive, and we know how my warrior feels about restrictions. So, I changed my major to sociology. This felt better, but what do I do with it? I knew I wanted to help people, but how? I thought about becoming a lawyer or psychologist, and finally I learned about social work. But I did not want to be one of those 'baby snatcher.' With further research and exploration, I learned what it meant to be a Social Worker. Wow! This is who I am anyway, I thought. I can get paid to 'help people'? What a world! So, the path narrows, and I'm feeling better about myself and the direction I want to go. But at home this baby is getting older and starting to talk, learn and have opinions of her own. My daughter is starting to notice and question me, the world, my behavior and my interactions with others. All of which starts to irritate the warrior side of me. While I'm busy busting my butt trying to be a better person, and earn a living for us, this kid is starting to get under my skin and my warrior is feeling unappreciated and disrespected. Not good. As I learned more about human behavior in sociology and psychology classes, I started to realize how damaged I was. The thing about some traumatic events is that the victims don't realize they were traumatizing, or wrong, until they're out of the situation. People in cults don't KNOW they're in a cult. They believe they are living the way

God intended. People in abusive relationships or abusive homes don't know that's abuse. They believe it's 'normal.' Until you know differently, physical, sexual, emotional or psychological abuse is 'just the way you grew up.' 'It's normal.' How many times have I said and heard that? But years later, and oceans away human behaviors and relationships and- "holy shit!"- that wasn't normal or right! So now I have to rethink my parenting and start a list of people I need to apologize to. Turns out being a calculating, careless, detached bitch is not good, or normal. Who knew right?

So, I stopped whipping, spanking, punishing or beating (pick one) my child, and started using alternative methods like; 'nurturing parenting, 'love and logic,' 'scream free' parenting. All of which take much longer than a good old fashion butt whippin'. This was an adjustment for both of us. There were times when I would say "I'm just gonna whip your butt 'cause I don't know what else to do." And other times when my daughter would beg me, saying "mommy please just whip my butt, I don't want to be in time-out." Eventually we figured it out. Probably with the arrival and help of my son. If she is my reason to live, and she is, then he is my reason to love. By the time my son came along, I had started questioning my tactics and actively working on being a better version of myself. I didn't want to live in a state of constant fear and anger. I tell people that my kids had two different mothers. My daughter got the crazy, ambitious and insecure version, and my son got the more aware and recovering version. With time, tears, humility, forgiveness, courage and love, they have grown me up. There is no doubt in my mind that I am a better person, and the world is a better place, because of my children. While I am still a work in progress, I am grateful for my Angels, teachers and Divine Grace. I am grateful for the ability and opportunity to teach and learn continuously the power of love, hope and healing posttraumatically.

This book is an attempt to help trauma survivors, and

caregivers, identify how and where the healing process is stuck, and ways to move through it. Because there is no getting over it, we *must* move through the pile of crap before real, and lasting, healing and growth can happen. And since you were not traumatized alone, you will not heal alone. The revelations in this book have come as a result of eighteen years of conscious personal and professional growth, observations and healing. These revelations have come up repeatedly, in sessions and in classes, when working with clients. Many are stuck and frustrated with their healing progress until they come to terms with these revelations. When they do, the change and growth is remarkable. At the end of each chapter, you will be invited to do some conscious observing of your own. There are some reflective questions designed to help you chart your own healing path and start to live again. There are no wrong answers. The idea is to explore and observe *without judgement, guilt or shame,* and record your findings for healing and recovery purposes.

I have learned that anyone with a heart can be traumatized. In or out of uniform, military or civilian; we all have loss and the need for love, hope and healing posttraumatically. Remember: trauma is about the loss of something important— the breaking of a trust, a sense of safety and wholeness. Trauma is a violation of a relationship between you and your sense of self it's a breaking of your personal sense of truth and safety. Accidental or intentional, trauma *always* leave a breach, that must be healed. An accidental punch still hurts. Healing the loss and filling the resulting void of trauma *will* require at least one other person. With respect, consistency and compassion, *terror, horror, helpless* and *hopeless* becomes *safety, validation, helpful* and *hopeful.* Let's start healing.

YOU ARE STILL ALIVE

This revelation may seem obvious, but for many trauma victims there is a sense of numb detachment from the body and the world. There's no denying that if you're reading this, you're alive; something you discovered (to your surprise) after your traumatizing event. I say surprise because that's what trauma is; a terrible, horrible, surprise that leaves you feeling helpless and hopeless. The perception of pending death or serious injury is part of the definition of being traumatized. This means that you truly believed that you would not survive. But you did. And depending on who you are and what happened to you, this can either be good news or bad news. Since this is your life and your journey, you get to decide how you want to feel about being alive after what you've been through.

What does it mean to be alive? It means that your heart is still beating, blood is flowing throughout your body, your brain, heart, lungs, kidneys and intestines are functioning. These are not things you have to 'make' happen; they're just happening. Being alive means you exist. It means you, like any other living thing, have the ability to grow, expand and change. Being alive is not the same as living. Being alive requires minimal, to no effort on your part, while living requires effort and courage. Living means intentionally interacting with your environment. It can take significant effort, and courage, to reengage with the world, with life, with people or with yourself. So, the revelation that you are still alive is a call to consciousness; a call to action, a call to that part of you that's not done yet; the part of you that survived the horror and wants to be more than its victim. I've seen people who were blown up, shot or beaten to the point of physical death; yet they are walking and talking. Some of these people find their new state of existence to be overwhelming and debilitating, and become stuck in a constant state of crisis, while others find a way to use this new form to learn, heal and teach themselves, and others, how to live again.

Living means choosing to interact with your environment. You choose to get out of bed. You choose to take a shower and get dressed. You choose to eat. You choose to go to work. You choose to interact with family and friends. You choose to date. You choose to be in an intimate relationship. You choose to become involved with coworkers, organizations or church. At the heart of any of these choices, is the decision to step outside of the fortress you created following your trauma. The choice to live again means having the courage to risk being seen, being touched, being cared for, being loved, being hurt, being betrayed and being safe again. Choosing to live again is choosing to stretch, expand and grow into the next best version of you. The risk is the possibility of losing it all again, but the reward is a stronger more conscious version of You. Essentially, choosing to live again means choosing to be the next best version of Yourself in the face of constant change and uncertainty. A caterpillar has no idea how to be a butterfly, and yet it does all it can do to live fully as a caterpillar. The result, is a gorgeous and healthy butterfly. So yes, you can do everything right, and still things will change. An acorn has no idea how to be an oak tree, and yet it sits in the dark earth, breaks apart, reaches for the light, stretches toward the sun, year after year; it breaks and stretches until it becomes a mighty oak tree. You are the one constant in your life! Wherever you go, there You are. You get to choose how you show up, over and over and over again, regardless of the situation.

Built into every living thing is the information, the essence, the knowing, of how to be the ultimate expression of itself. What sets us apart from all other living things, is cognition, judgement and choice. We think; We judge; We Choose. This process slows us down, and can stop us all together, on the journey to becoming the next best version of ourselves. Ironically, the very part of us that makes us 'evolved humans,' can also make us behave as though we are untamed animals...lurking in the shadows, at the mercy of our environment, isolated, defensive, aggressive, shy, suspicious and unapproachable; all because we *think* this will keep us safe. Posttraumatically, our cognition, judgment and choices are made from a trauma victims' perspective. Trauma is a horrible surprise that rewires our information circuits to the point of *disorder.* Trauma changes everything! How you see, how you hear, how you feel, how you taste and how you smell, are all changed. Consequently, all that matters, is never being surprised again. In this state, living doesn't seem like an option; only surviving. To heal from the wounds of horror and terror, victims must make the choice to live. Otherwise they will remain stuck on the posttraumatic rollercoaster, reliving the traumas over, and over again. Every breath, every minute, every hour and every day, is a chance to start over. Your life; your choice.

Think about who you were before the traumatic event, or events, that you have survived. Think about the person you were before all hell broke loose, and you believed you were 'done.'

Pause.

Now, think about who you are now. What has life been like since you were traumatized? What is your life like now? *Pause.*

Now, think about who you want to be. Try to imagine what you would do if fear was not an option. What would you do if you could not fail? What small steps can you take toward the person you want to be? These steps can be as small as getting out of bed, taking a shower, having a meal, calling a supportive person, leaving your house, taking a walk or even brushing your teeth. Depending on where you are on your journey, the steps will vary. The step doesn't matter as much as the choice to move. On the following pages, I invite you to write (without judgement) about what you would do if you could not fail and steps you can take now toward who you want to be. No step is too small, and no goal is too big.

Notes

Notes

WHILE YOU WERE OUT,
SOMETHING KEPT YOU ALIVE

This revelation may be off putting for some, so bear with me. Whether you're a scientist, atheist, agnostic, spiritual or religious person, your body experienced an event that disrupted your state of consciousness. Regardless of what you believe in, something bigger, stronger and smarter than you— call it God, Universe, Elohim, Jesus, Yeshuah, Spirit, Buddha, Allah or Energy; it kept you alive when you thought you were going to die. That's what trauma is; an event so overwhelming to the senses that your brain believes death, or serious harm, is imminent and the body prepares to die. But you don't. Instead your body freezes, for seconds, minutes, hours, days, weeks or even months depending on the physical impact of the traumatic event. This 'freeze' is the third step in the body's stress response following 'fight' and 'flight.' While you were frozen or dissociated, your body continued to record the details of the event, its surroundings, the sights, sounds, smells, tests and sensations. So, that when you regained consciousness, you could collect this information and decide what to do with it. What happened? Who can I call? Where am I? When am I? Can anybody, see or hear me? These questions fire rapidly and are answered at varying speeds depending on the circumstances of your specific event. Are you in a crowd, in a home, on the side of a road, in the woods, on a battle field, in an abandoned building, in a hospital or in a movie theatre? Is it day or night? As answers start to flow and you become more physically stable, more questions arise. What do I do now? How do I move forward? Can I move forward? How did I survive? What will my life look like now? How can I face myself? How can I face my family? What will they think of me? What do I think of myself? What do I need? What do I want? What matters now? Does anyone care about what happened to me? Do I care about myself? The answers to these questions can move you forward and set you free or hold you hostage making you a prisoner.

You don't have to instruct a physical wound to heal. You just need to keep it clean, supported and protected, and the body is designed to do the healing work—swelling to reduce movement, pain to remind you to be careful and slow down, clotting to create a scab and so on. Your body can rebuild bone! And given the right support, our hearts and minds will heal and rebuild as well. The Intelligence that keeps you alive, beats your heart, heals your paper cuts, grows your hair and blinks your eye, guarantees it. You don't need to pay heart rent, blood mortgage or bone insurance; it's taken care of—provided. We just need to give our broken hearts and minds the same attention we give to our broken bones.

Imagine, how different life would be, if we could see the extent of our mental and emotional wounds. How would we behave, if there were casts, splints or cutches for our hearts and minds following a traumatic event? Would we be as considerate as we are for someone with crutches and a broken leg trying to navigate stairs or tight spaces? If we could see the emotional wounds of the crash or explosion that may have caused the physical damage, how would we interact? Would we slow down the flow of information the way we hold the door and the elevator? Would we offer to repeat or rephrase instructions or requests, the way we offer to carry a bag or box? Would we be more attentive to the psychological and emotional wounds that may accompany a black eye or concussion, or do we need a back story? Does it matter if the person with the back eye and concussion is a service member, boxer, football player or domestic violence victim? Regardless of the source of trauma, our bodies behave much the same way when traumatized; shock is shock, pain is pain, loss is loss. Judgement, guilt and shame that follow the event will, unfortunately, determine the extent of support given to the individual and the resulting wounds. The ability, and right, to heal and grow posttraumatically, is built into every living being. Love and support is all that's required from us. The Intelligence that kept you alive when you were unconscious or 'blacked out,' is always active; always supporting growth and healing. We may not agree on what 'It' is, but we know It's there.

Giving yourself permission to heal is the first step. This means surrendering to the power and wisdom that created you. Permission to heal is about getting out of your own way and letting yourself be, supported, cared for and loved. You don't have to believe in a creator or higher power to heal; your skin and bones do it by design. The power that beats your heart isn't conditionally distributed; it is ever present. We've come to expect that our bones and skin will repair themselves. So, we do what we can to support them and go on—a band aid, a splint, ice, rest, elevate and so on; maybe checking in with the doctor in six to eight weeks. That's faith. Based on years of evidence, we now take for granted that the body will heal. Miracles are only miracles until we understand what's happening. Once we can explain how and why bone and skin repair themselves, it stops being wonderous. Once we had machines powerful enough to make the invisible visible we stopped calling them miracles. We simply support the wounds and expect the healing.

But there seems to be a disconnect where wounded hearts

and minds are concerned. Support is still too slow. As if nothing *really* happened; we avoid, delay and deny our emotional wounds. So common, and dismissive, is the attitude toward mental and emotional damage, that the sayings 'you're fine,' 'you just want attention,' 'you'll get over it,' or 'don't dwell on it' become internalized by the victim. The emotional and psychological wounds become more about the maladaptive behaviors than the actual traumatic events themselves. Trauma survivors tend to blame themselves for the 'mess' they're in or blame others for causing them to behave in destructive ways. Either way, attention is given to the behaviors resulting from the traumatic event, instead of the wounds driving the behaviors. Wounded beings behave differently than healed beings. Man, woman, child, lion, cub, elephant, dog, cat or rabbit will behave aggressively, defensively and withdrawn when traumatized. These behaviors are attempts to feel safe, even when help is being offered, the wounded may recoil or attack. So, care and support must be compassionate and nonjudgmental—as neutral as a heartbeat. When we focus more on behaviors than we do the traumatic loss, malpractice/maltreatment can occurs.

There is the attitude that we're somehow stuck with labels like Anxiety, Depression, Bipolar, Borderline Personality, Obsessive Compulsive or Posttraumatic Stress Disorders. As if they are things! They are labels (judgments) given to a list of behaviors, no more, and no less! They are medical identifiers given to trauma survivors who are trying to stabilize (or feel 'normal again') posttraumatically. And each one of these behaviors are because of some significant loss. They are the response to losing an important thing or person; they are attempts to cope with the life changing event that was determined, by the *individual*, to be traumatic, overwhelming, catastrophic or just too much to handle. Losing a family member, a friend, a job, a home or a body part are all potential causes for a trauma response. The word trauma comes from the Greek word meaning serious wounded needing professional attention. A wound leaves damage that must be repaired, if the wounded is expected to regain full functioning. The posttraumatic emotional and psychological loss felt by a person following a catastrophic or traumatic loss is personal and unique to that individual. The damage and trauma response are directly correlated to the significance placed on the loss by the person experiencing it—trauma is subjectively registered in and by the individual.

No one has the right, nor the authority, to tell a trauma survivor how he or she feels Posttraumatically. No one has the right to tell a survivor to 'just get over it.' Even if you have your own trauma history, it does not give you the right or authority to tell someone else how to experience their trauma. The significance of the loss, is determined by the individual losing the significant thing, and *not* the grown-up or 'expert' professional, witnessing it. Another important element of trauma is that it is *subjective, subjective, subjective!* That means it is based on the individual's perception of the experience.

What makes it seem so common is the symptoms and behaviors that follow. We are all created the same, and yet we are all different; like snowflakes, apple trees, butterflies, ocean waves or roses, we are commonly unique. We are the same in that we all bleed, cry, mourn, yell, laugh, fear, attack, defend and protect. What makes us different is why and how we do these things. Our values and perspectives will determine what we do, when, why and how we do it following a loss. Faith in science, or faith in a higher power, is a value that we learn and use to make sense of our world, and our place in it. Our values are how we make sense and relate to our world—ourselves and those we care for. Any threat, real or perceived can cause a defensive response. Any loss, real or perceived can trigger a trauma response. And trauma is experienced, and responded to, from a primitive, instinctive and irrational part of ourselves. When we believe our life is endangered, we don't think. We act. We act from a place of raw, primitive emotional instinct. Posttraumatic—after a traumatic experience, we try to 'make sense' of the event and our response to it. The ability, and willingness, to do this with compassion will make all the difference. Cognition, logic, judgement, guilt, shame and punishment will most certainly slow down the healing process; because, trauma is beyond cognition and logic, which is what makes it a disgusting surprise. Trauma is an event that is beyond belief, outside of our current sense of reality, that leaves us feeling helpless and hopeless to prevent it from happening.

When we attempt to rationalize the invisible, we discount important information, which results in long, and unnecessary, pain and suffering. When we label mental and emotional wounds using only scientific evidence, the person is lost to the disease. There is no x-ray for a broken heart or shattered mind, only the feelings and meaning we give to the experience. There are instruments that can measure the effects of trauma on the physical brain such as; SPEC or PET scans (methods used to examine chemical damage in the brain and other soft tissue in the body), and they are often too expensive for most people to afford. And they cannot identify *meaning* or *value*, two inexplicable ingredients of trauma—as it is the loss of something or someone meaningful, and the value of the thing or person lost, that facilitate the conditions for a trauma response. If you're not a cat or dog person, you'll respond quite differently to the death of a cat or dog than someone who is. If you didn't know Jim from Iowa, you won't miss him like his family or friends will. The emotional damage that results from trauma is rarely seen, believed or understood—the very things needed to heal from trauma.

Scientifically, yes. These diagnoses result from some chemical imbalance and can be treated with chemicals—partly true. We are chemical/hormonal beings and can be treated with artificial chemicals and hormones to help us feel balanced—also, partly true. We are walking masses of cells—also partly true. And then, we are simply energy vibrating at a frequency slow enough that we are visible to one another—also partly true. Pick a truth and you are partly right. But if you're trying to heal the entire being, all parts must be addressed. All behaviors and symptoms must be examined and treated using multiple methods. Which might explain why most hospital have a place to pray, or why many insurance companies are starting to pay for 'holistic' or 'alternative' healing practices. The marriage of faith and science is becoming more common place. Which hopefully means we are getting enough proof that our hearts and minds can, and will, heal when given care, support, and the same faith given to the healing of broken bones.

Knowing and believing what is possible can be difficult for some people and impossible for others. The field of psychology is new, when compared to other sciences. It has struggled to fine its validity and establish support for itself in a world of concrete, proof and fact driven funding as it tries to conceptualize 'the mind' or define 'a thought' or 'a feeling.' As I stated before, there is no x-ray for a broken heart nor an MRI for a psychotic break. The field of neuroscience shows great promise in combining Knowing with knowing. While there are devices to examine and measure chemical imbalances and soft tissue damage, the emotional history and experience remains subjective and beyond current scientific examination or explanation. There is only the behaviors and attempted explanations of the emotions and thoughts driving these behaviors; all based on meaning and values assigned to the loss by the survivor. Currently, professionals and caregivers must rely on the guidance of the trauma survivors. All of whom can only give their subjective opinion of what they believe is happening. The 'D' in every 'disorder' is very much about *disorganized* information. Disorganized should never be mistaken for stupidity! Trauma survivors are not stupid or crazy, they are sporadically lost in their trauma history. And how we respond to this misinformation or missed information will send survivors down a path to healing or more pain and suffering. Trauma shatters our sense of safety, our sense of place, time and space in the world. Posttraumatic communication can be frustrating for both the sender and receiver of information. Trauma survivors tend to communicate in pieces; so that times, events, locations and emotions are often incongruent. This broken communication can cause anger, frustration, mistrust, fear and abandonment for both the trauma survivors and the caregivers. I've heard many survivors say, "I can't talk to people without feeling stupid," "I can't make sense of this" or "I just blacked out and forgot where I was" or "I must be crazy," or "I must sound like an idiot." On the other hand, I've heard many caregivers say, "he's always lying and making up stories," or "he just explodes for no reason" or "he conveniently forgets the important stuff" or "he just doesn't care" or "she's just trying to get attention" or "she's being dramatic again." So, in this state of *disorganized* information, victims, survivors and caregivers must be willing to practice compassionate witnessing, compassionate support with self and others. From what the trauma survivor perceives, to what the healer and caregiver believe; all must be considered in order to achieve the ultimate goal, of healing and growth, posttraumatically. A wise man once said, "According to your faith be it done to you" Mat 9:29. I take this to mean, whatever you believe to be true, you get to be right. How you view a situation and what you expect to find, you will find. Call it miracle or call it science; there are countless stories of patients healing and recovering, and doctors and professional are speechless to explain it. I'm sure the first time a bone healed it was considered a 'miracle.' Now it's just expected. Faith, "...is being sure of what you hope for and certain of what you do not see" Heb 11:1. What do you hope for? What do you believe?

Which brings us back to the something that kept you

alive. Whatever It is, It continues to work with or without your acknowledgement. It doesn't need your help or permission to heal you. You only need to support, trust and allow. Scientist, priests, shaman, mothers and doctors regardless of religious stance, all know that there is something that heals and works to keep us alive. Some call it time; as in 'give it time, it'll be ok,' 'time heals all wounds,' or come back and see me in 6 weeks' time.' Time doesn't heal anything. Healing just happens. Like planets move without crashing into each other. It happens as part of Divine Design. Whenever something is damaged, broken or wounded it is healed. How functional the broken thing, or person is following the damage, is determined by the attention, support and love it receives. If a broken tree branch is taped and anchored, it heals straight. If a broken bone is reset and supported, it heals straight. If a person is supported and nurtured after an emotional loss, the heart and mind recover. If there is no support, healing will still occur, but there will be funky and interesting quarks, bends, curves…'character' where the damage occurred; much like those intriguing trees you find that were struck by lightning. So that now, the tree has an interesting bend in the damaged branch. The person with the broken bone now walks with a limp, and the person with the broken heart now interacts weird or differently in social and personal relationships. We've all heard of a relative's 'trick knee, hip or ankle; or the relative that acts weird or withdrawn.' So, the Something that keeps us alive, is always working. Ours is to work with It, for optimal recovery. Get the surgery when needed, get the cast when needed, go to physical therapy when need, and go to mental and emotional therapy when needed. Get the support needed to trust and allow optimal healing. I love this quote from Dr. Caroline Myss.

> "We are not meant to stay wounded. We are supposed to move though our tragedies and

challenges and to help each other move through the many painful episodes of our lives. By remaining stuck in the power of our wounds, we block our own transformation. We overlook the greater gifs inherent in our wounds—the strength to overcome them and the lessons that we are meant to receive through them. Wounds are the means through which we enter the hearts of other people. They are meant to teach us to become compassionate and wise."

Depending on where you are in your healing journey, you may not want to hear this. And that's ok. Knowing where you are, is just as important as knowing where you want to go. The path to healing always starts where you are. And the choice to move is always yours. The Something that kept you alive is always there. Much like the electricity in your home, you just have to flick a switch. The choice to be an active participant in your healing is always available to you. Just "ask and you will receive; seek and you will find; knock and the door will open." Matthew 7:7. You much ASK. You must flick the switch. The wisdom that beats your heart waits for you in the stillness to quiet yourself and listen.

What do you believe? What are you seeking? What keeps you alive? What heals you? Is it faith, science, or something else? *Pause.*

Think about what you have been taught and what you now believe about yourself, a Higher Power or Something Bigger than yourself. What is it in you that moves you forward? There are no wrong answers to these questions. On the following pages, you are invited to write down whatever thoughts or feelings that come to mind and heart for you as you ask these questions. Let your mind wander through your life experiences and notice what questions, answers and feelings come up for you. Without judgement, just notice how your mind, body and heart respond to the above questions, and write down your findings.

Notes

Notes

THERE IS NO 'BACK TO NORMAL'

This revelation can be both freeing and frustrating. You have a choice to either start over willingly, or you can feel forced to let go of the past. Because of your traumatic event, you are forever changed. There can be a *new* normal, or a new life, but you can never go back to the person you were before. You cannot 'unknow' what you now know. You cannot unsee, unhear, unfeel, untaste or unsmell anything about that event. As a result of your traumatic event, your entire body has been changed, on a cellular level. The egg has been cracked! It's as if you were remade, reprogrammed or reborn, and you get to decide what the rest of your new life will look like. Baby chick or raw egg; either way the shell is broken, and there is no back to 'normal.' There is no uncracking or unbreaking the egg. There is a new version of you waiting for you to decide what happens next. Uncertainty is valid and should be expected. Good news, you've already been to hell. You've already survived the darkest, lowest, horrifying, terrifying event of your life. Better news, there's nowhere else to go but up. Broken is not destroyed. Every advancement followed a hindrance; every success followed a failure; every birth followed a death; and every trauma can precede a new life. In the posttraumatic mess, are all the ingredients needed for the new you to emerge. You've been rearranged on a cellular level (mentally, physically and emotionally), and you now have what it takes to not only survive, but to expand into the next best version of yourself. While you may not know how yet, it is possible. You are still here; but you've been rearranged and have had some new information added. You have been forever changed, and with these changes come new possibilities, options, demands and expectations and potential freedoms.

This is a new you; which means, you have NEVER been in THIS situation before. Not unlike a newborn baby, you are new to the world and the world is now new to you. You see with new eyes. You hear with new ears. You touch with new hands. You speak and taste with a new tongue. You smell with a new nose. You love with a new heart. Every relationship in your life must be reevaluated. Your relationships with parents, spouse, siblings, children, school, work, and most importantly yourself, are all new. To the extent that you are willing, and able, to truly accept and understand this truth, you will heal and recover more easily than if you resist and insist on forcing your old life, old dreams, old expectations and your old demands to fit into your 'new' life. Because cognition, judgement and choice are both assets and liabilities, permission to heal posttraumatically is the secret to living your new life.

By permission I mean, accepting the new you without judgment, guilt or shame— which are the barriers to true and lasting healing. Give yourself the time, love and attention that you would give to a newborn baby. This is not to suggest that you are dumb or stupid in anyway (something most trauma survivors believe about themselves); you are not! It is an invitation to be as compassionate and patient as possible with the new you. It is an invitation to be as attentive to yourself as you would be to a newborn. There is no way you could have prepared for, or prevented, the traumatic event. I'll repeat that. There is no way you could have prepared for, or prevented, the traumatic event. If you could have, it would not have been traumatizing. As I mentioned before, trauma is a disgusting surprise, that occurs when the brain and body agree that the situation is *terrifying, horrifying,* and you are *helpless* and *hopeless* to prevent it. Knowing, believing and understanding this is crucial to the healing process.

In addition to the new you, you now have a newly awakened lifelong companion. Some call it monster, guardian, warrior, beast, gate keeper, devil, animal, demon, protector, destroyer, the list goes on. What it is, regardless of your judgement, is the physical part of you that kept you alive—your warrior self. This companion is the physical part of you that took over and did whatever was necessary for your survival; it did what was needed in that moment, to save your life. When you froze (because fight and flight were not possible), your warrior self took over and saved you from the horror and terror of whatever traumatic event occurred. You may not approve of how he or she handled the situation, and you now have the luxury of judging, after the fact (not fair!). You may be ashamed or grateful for this part of yourself, depending on where you are on your healing journey. Many trauma survivors are afraid and ashamed of this part of themselves. They try to run from it by frequently changing jobs or locations, hide from it by isolating/withdrawing, deny it with drugs, drown it with alcohol or kill it with suicide attempts. These forms of prolonged suffering can be significantly diminished with care, support and understanding of this warrior part of yourself. This part of you cannot be destroyed without killing yourself. It was born to protect you!! It was born the second you felt horrified, terrified, helpless and hopeless. It was born the moment you felt too overwhelmed. And its only purpose, while misguided sometimes, is to protect you. It wants to make sure you never feel unsafe again. And it will remain in control of your life until you find the courage to live again.

While you can never get rid of this companion, you can control him or her. You control this part of yourself by validating, acknowledging and accepting who and what it is—your warrior self. In a word, collaboration. You may even want to thank him or her for doing the dirty work of surviving the horror. And then reassure it that you are strong enough now to protect and manage yourself, and your environment. This managing can feel like a full-time job; because posttraumatically you are constantly on guard—hypervigilant for any possible threat. This constant scanning for danger is exhausting! It takes your time and attention away from everything! Personal and professional relationships suffer because of this distraction. You spend all of your time paying partial attention to school, work, family, friends and yourself. Consequently, you have difficulty remembering, learning, engaging, sleeping, eating or just sitting calmly; all of which leads to irritability, agitation, sadness, anxiety, defensiveness, anger, frustration, explosions, isolation and so on. Until finally, something happens, and you say the magic words, and the 'beast, warrior, monster...' is unleashed.

For many combat veterans, the magic words are "fuck it." For many civilian survivors, the magic word is "whatever" or "forget it." Regardless of your status, these words translate to 'I'm done', 'I can't do this' or 'I'm overwhelmed;' triggering a sense of helplessness and hopelessness, and the feeling of being threatened or attacked. Many survivors describe this as a 'blackout.' In this state, the warrior takes over and destruction follows. The warriors' only purpose is to protect you from any, and all danger, real or imagined. This can be expressed as an explosion, or an implosion, depending on your coping strategies. If you are more inclined toward action or anxiety, an explosive response is most likely. In this case, there's often a physical or verbal attack on a person or property. There can be a verbal attack where you berate family members, friends, spouse, coworkers, clerks, strangers and even telephone representatives. Whoever happens to be present, the moment you decide 'I'm done,' and the warrior takes control, gets it. It can also be a physical attack where you beat the living crap out of someone or destroy anything you can get your hands on; with the extreme being homicide. However, if you are more inclined toward withdrawal and depression, an implosive response is most likely. In this case, there is often self-deprecation and self-harming. This too, can be verbal or physical. This can sound like, I'm so stupid, so dumb, so weak, so pathetic, so worthless and I don't deserve this job, this person, this life. It can also look like cutting, overdosing, suicide attempts and various other risky behaviors; with the extreme being completed suicide.

Either way there's an assault, due to your perception of danger and feeling threatened by something or someone in your environment. Real or imagined doesn't matter; all that matters in that moment is your perception. And when you say the 'magic words...' A grocery store clerk, a VA representative, a security guard, a clueless driver cutting you off, a waitress bumping into you, a playful child jumping on your back, a flirtatious partner coming up behind you, a missed appointment, a missed assignment, the tone of a voice or the look of something suspicious, or just the sight, sound, smell or taste of something that reminds you of your traumatic event. Any, all, or a combination of these can be enough for you to say the 'magic words.' And it's as if you throw your hands up, leave the driver's seat and sit in a passenger seat of your bus; which immediately signals your warrior to take over. And without hesitation, he or she does. And being your unconditional protector, your warrior doesn't need much justification for a defensive attack. It loves a good challenge!

The warrior is constantly on guard. You can imagine a restless lion or tiger pacing back and forth in the background; always waiting for an opportunity to pounce. Or a restless fighter waiting outside the rink for his or her match to start. Like a personal bodyguard strapped to your back 24/7, your warrior stands ready. Its lifelong mission is keeping you alive.

This is important to understand, because this part of you is never going away. It was awakened the moment you felt terror, horror, helpless and hopeless; whether you could verbalize it or not. As a hungry neglected baby, an abandoned child, an abused child, a rape victim, a robbery victim, a child of divorced or of deceased parents, a service member on your first deployment, a victim of an earthquake, flood or hurricane survivor. Regardless of the event, the moment you were forced out of *your* sense of safety, your warrior was awakened. And has grown with every traumatic event you've ever experienced. We all have one. Every single one of us has a warrior! The size and ferocity of this warrior depends on each person's trauma history.

If you were raised in a palace or mansion and was catered to, protected, supported and wanted for nothing, your warrior is most likely a cute little carefree cub. But if you were raised in an environment where survival was uncertain or by broken adults with unresolved trauma histories of their own (alcoholic, drug addict, war veteran, rape victim...), your warrior is most likely a full grown hungry beast that demands constant attention, validation and respect. Neither one is bad or good; both have their place. But the care instructions are significantly different for one, then for the other. Survival is a full-time job and so is living. Both require constant attention and intention. Nothing in civilian or 'normal' life can compare to the rush of battle for a warrior, nothing! Its only purpose is survival—winning. So, finding appropriate challenges for your warrior must become a significant part of your healing strategy.

Adrenaline is possibly the most addictive substance on the planet, and the body makes it naturally. It is our action drug/ hormone. Adrenaline prepares the body to fight or flight. It also gives us the energy to work, play and have sex. The body will produce as much as it needs to manage the perceived level of impending stress, to the point of 'blackout,' or freeze. Once the body is flooded with a high enough dose of adrenaline, you freeze, dissociate, blackout or pass out. This is when either the warrior takes over or you are physically incapacitated. For trauma survivors, there is a continuously high level of adrenaline flowing, fueling the hypervigilance. There is a constant restlessness that must be addressed and managed. The warrior hungers for battle. By this I mean a challenge. The high levels of adrenaline must be exerted and burned off. This is our action hormone and if no action is taken, disorder and chaos follow.

So, it is important to know your warrior. Give it the respect and acknowledgement it deserves. Find ways to challenge your warrior. Organize your days, weeks, months, life, in a structured orderly fashion. Remember, trauma is a surprising event that shatters your sense of safety. It destroys your sense of normal, leaving chaos and disorder behind. Lasting healing and recovery must include a sense of structured order, and predictability—a routine of some sort. Again, like a baby that needs a consistent feeding, changing and sleeping schedule, the new you needs a sense of predictability to feel safe. Structure, and predictability is what makes all successful organizations and relationships work. Of course, in this structured order, adjustments are made as growth and healing progress. For the action-oriented warriors, try physical challenges—gym, hikes, camping, marathons, wilderness excursions, survival courses, boxing, martial arts, rock and mountain climbing, and then teaching these to others. For the introspective warriors, try mental challenges—learning new languages, earning various degrees, painting, crafting, writing, travel, pottery, creating and then teaching these to others. Your warrior is a lifelong partner and living a 'normal' or productive life, depends on your ability, and willingness, to collaborate with him or her. Your new normal must include a productive partnership with your warrior. We all need a purpose, a goal, a reason to show up physically, mentally and emotionally. If he/she is not at peace, neither are you and vice versa. If you're anxious, lonely, depressed or angry, your warrior is on guard; ready to equalize/stabilize the situation. This is survival stance. However, if you're content, happy, productive and encouraged, your warrior is relaxed and trusting you to manage things. This is a living stance. Surviving and living are equally demanding of your time and energy but have very differ consequences.

Surviving is primarily crisis management and short-term planning. If you are in survival mode, you probably spend most of your time reacting to your environment—most likely you feel at the mercy of an unsafe world. In survivor mode, the world is a battle field, the warrior is in the driver's seat and you are somewhere in the back of your bus trying to decide if or when you'll start living again. While living, on the other hand, is submerging into the present experience and long-term planning. If you are in living mode, the world is wondrous, and you are interacting with your environment, exploring possibilities. You are engaged in personal and social relationships; trusting and planning with flexibility. In living mode, you tend to plan vacations, parties or weekend getaways; you probably spend most of the time proactively observing and experiencing your environment—most likely you are in the driver's seat and your warrior is resting, relaxed in the back of your bus.

So, your *new* normal must involve a collaboration between the two of you. He or She is not a negotiator! That's your work. Managing yourself and your environment is about knowing who you are, what you need, what you value and who you can trust. There is a valid time and place for every emotion you have. Your new life depends on you mastering these emotions and using them as motivation to create the next best version of You. Every emotion is a message. Every sensation in your body has information that can communicate to you who you are, and what is important to you. From a simple growling in your stomach that says I'm hungry or a bump from a stranger in the grocery store, to the loss of a job or a persistent headache that says I have a tumor. All of these are sensations that convey messages that solicits a response from you. Denying your feelings only sets the stage for your warrior self to take over. When too much time has passed from the initial message of need, to the corresponding fulfilment of that need, the warrior feels justified in taking action. If you ignore the message of 'I'm hungry,' 'I'm disrespected,' 'I'm unimportant,' 'I'm tired,' or 'I'm lonely,' you are risking the "righteous," yet destructive response of your warrior; because he or she is *always* keeping score. The warrior notes every time you ignore your needs for something or someone else; regardless of the reason. Normal, happy living doesn't mean problem free. Life is full of twists and turns. That you are reading this book, at this moment in your life, is an indication that you know this to be true, on some level. It also means that you are interested in learning how to navigate these twists and turns more constructively. Managing your warrior is a crucial part of that.

This means learning who you really are, what you value, what gives you a sense of purpose/meaning. It means learning to trust yourself and others again, and creating strong networks of support. Your warrior is formidable and sometimes misguided; it is protective and defensive with little regard for social appropriateness. Warriors are not nurturers. They are not concerned with wives, husbands, children, family and friends. Warriors are interested in winning! Husbands, wives, mothers, fathers, sisters, brothers and civilians are concerned with relationships—not warriors. Warriors are lone survivors. Knowing the difference between your warrior self, and your social self, is the most important thing when attempting to create a support network. This 'protector' is hypervigilant and hyperaware of anything that *seems* to be *potentially* dangerous— it doesn't have to be a real danger. For a warrior, everything and everyone is suspect. Which means that anything that is different, anything that is related to your traumatic event, or anything related to being vulnerable in any way, is suspect and cause for alarm. Left unchecked, your warrior will destroy any attempts at a personal relationship. This is why getting care, support, information and treatment is so important. Too many trauma survivors end up alone because they never learned to trust again, themselves or anyone else. I've said it before, and it bears repeating, *you didn't get traumatized alone, and you will not heal alone.* The warrior believes he's alone, he needs no one, and she trusts no one, and she never sleeps. So, to regain control of your life and relationships, you must be willing to work as hard, if not harder, than the wounded part of yourself to create your new 'normal.' This requires an ongoing conversation between you and your warrior self. It means constantly reassuring him or her that you are now willing, and able, to face stressful or challenging situations in a constructive and productive manner. It means constantly communicating to your warrior that stress doesn't always mean danger. Warriors tend to think in extremes—black or white, wrong or right, with me or against me, friend or enemy, good or bad, success or failure. There is no in between for warriors. Relationship requires the allowance for grays, maybes, sometimes, associates, and possibilities. Instead of the all or nothing thinking of the survivor's stance; you must develop a sort of structured flexibility. Relationship requires patience and diplomacy (two things warriors tend to lack).

Your ability to effectively survey and assess a situation, and then communicating that to your warrior self, will directly affect how you reconnect to yourself and the world around you. Many trauma survivors don't remember what it feels like to be in their bodies. They don't remember how sober, hunger, rest, peace, happiness, love or trust feels. For far too long, and for far too many, all that is known is numbness, anger, fear, suspicion, sadness, dread and defensiveness. I have many survivors tell me that they have no idea how their bodies feel.

There is a disconnect from the self posttraumatically, that can grow into a disconnect from the world. This disconnection strengthens and encourages the warrior self; it gives him or her a stronger sense of purpose and entitlement. If you are going to regain your sense of self, and purpose, you must be willing to take control of yourself, your emotions and your life. Not to be confused with controlling your environment; but controlling yourself, and how you show up in your environment. You cannot always control other people, or how things show up in your life. You can bully and manipulate people, but not for long. Everyone has free will. Everyone! We are all born with it. And no one's desires gets to supersede another's indefinitely. I often tell people, to try feeding a new born who is not hungry. You can't. A new born baby will refuse to suckle, if it is not hungry—a perfect example of free will. This act of refusal is not an act of rebellion or disrespect; it's just an expression of the baby's current condition—not hungry. You cannot force your will on to someone else and expect to be free and happy. You cannot imprison or enslave someone without also imprisoning or enslaving yourself. Flexible collaboration with yourself and others in your environment will get you to where you want to be. That means patience, compassion, forgiveness and respect. It means giving yourself and others the benefit of doubt.

Sadly, many trauma survivors become both the prisoner and the warden in their own lives—stuck in a trap of self-loathing and punishment. Without judgment, without guilt and without shame, work with your warrior. With love and respect, acknowledge his or her hard work, and efforts, to keep you safe and alive. Reassure him or her that you can, and will, keep yourself safe. This again, will take a lot of your time and attention; because again, the warrior doesn't sleep. He or she is always ready to protect and defend you. So, compromise doesn't happen easily, and the warrior will not tolerate injustice; remember his score keeping. Living in a less than honorable way will alarm him or her, and will not be tolerated for long. Again, ignoring your physical, mental and emotional needs are all forms of injustice. Anything that deprives you of yours sense of peace, and safety, can trigger your warrior.

For example, allowing someone to take advantage of you, betray you or cheat you in anyway, will get the warrior's attention. For instance, someone borrows money and doesn't pay it back, someone zooms into your parking spot, someone yells at you for something that wasn't your fault, someone takes your lunch, you're passed over for a deserved promotion, you're lied to about anything or you're falsely accused of something, and so on. Any perceived unjust act will alarm your warrior. If you don't self-advocate and address the situation when it happens, the warrior starts pacing and tallying this score. Anger, agitation, irritability, sadness and rumination start to build up inside of you. These little occurrences may not matter individually, but as they add up, your stress level is raised, your adrenaline increases, and your warrior becomes increasingly restless. Until finally feeling powerless and disrespected, you're 'done' and you say the 'magic words,' leave the driver's seat of your bus, and the warrior takes over. Unfortunately, more often than not, the explosion occurs with a 'final straw,' but has the wrath for an entire bale of hay. And usually toward some unsuspecting undeserving bystander; like a friend or family member and is followed by feelings of guilt and shame. So, continued communication between you, your warrior and your environment is key to getting, and keeping, your new 'normal' moving forward. If you can justify the perceived injustice, if you can explain, get an explanation or an apology for why you were 'disrespected,' something like "oh I'm sorry I didn't see you there," or "sorry you didn't get the promotion, John was more qualified because...," or "sorry I missed your call sweetie, I was in a meeting, or my phone died," or "I'll get something to eat right after this meeting." If the warrior has an explanation for your discomfort, and a justified explanation for the perceived wrong, he or she will calm down and trust you to handle things—until you don't.

I have worked with countless trauma survivors who insist on punishing and condemning the traumatized parts of themselves—calling him or her 'dumb, stupid, crazy and weak.' When I ask them to imagine a friend or a family member in the same situation, they all state that they would never say these things to anyone else. My next question is, then why do you say these things to, and about, yourself? Judging and punishing yourself, or anyone, for the choices made prior to, and during, the traumatic event based on information gathered after the traumatic event, is just wrong. It's mean and unfair. If you had more information, time, or resources at the time of the traumatic event, you would have used them. This posttraumatic judging feeds the guilt and the shame that is the poison preventing trauma wounds from healing. Your warrior lives to protect you, even from yourself. So, in the misguided attempt to make you feel safe, he or she will respond to these negative feelings with countless defenses, like anger, sadness, isolation, withdrawal, addictions and in some cases homicide and or suicide. Collaboration is a requirement to move toward your new 'normal.' Healing is just on the other side of the wall of judgment, guilt and shame. And your warrior is going with you as well. You get to decide how.

What are your triggers? What are the things that make you angry, sad, anxious and depressed? What sounds, sights, smells, tastes and textures get you upset? Do you know the difference between you and your warrior self?

Pause.

Think about how you interact with people when you feel happy and safe? Think about times when you shut down or blacked out? What changes caused the differences? What are some small, activities you can start doing on a regular basis to develop a sense of routine and safety? On the next pages, you are invited to write down your triggers, if you know them, or patterns of mood and behavioral changes. No trigger or cause is too big or too small. Just write down things that you've noticed that change your mood and the way you show up. What activities challenge your warrior, and give him or her a sense of accomplishment? How can you reward completion of these challenges?

Notes

Notes

Notes

THERE IS NO EXPIRATION
DATE FOR TRAUMA

Trauma wounds can wait indefinitely to be validated and healed. This revelation may feel somewhat unnerving, if not outright infuriating. To know that your personal *hell* sits, and waits for you can provoke varying emotions. Emotions, the very thing trauma survivors spend a lifetime trying to avoid. Avoidance, withdrawing, numbing, isolating or running from feelings and memories are hallmark behaviors of PTSD, Anxiety and Depression. But bear with me. Medically, trauma means wound; wound means a breach in the integrity of the skin. This can be a scratch, a scrape, a stab, a gunshot, or the loss of a limb. Psychologically, trauma means shocking violation to the psyche. This can be the experience of, or witness to, an offensive word, a slap, a punch, a severe beating, a robbery, an earthquake, gun battle, or an explosion. Regardless of the source, there is the loss of a sense of safety. A loss in the previous state of wholeness. The breach, breaking, cracking or shattering, of the victim's psychological wholeness, must be repaired! If not, the physical/psychological wound with fester, leaks, oozes, and bleeds all over your life. Infection, mood disturbance, sleep disturbance, fever, irrational behaviors, destructive behaviors, isolation, withdrawal, memory loss, learning disability, eating and digestive disorders, emotional and psychological disorders can all be symptoms of both physical and psychological traumas. What happens in the body chemically, following a traumatic event is life changing, and must be given the attention needed to heal.

Because trauma happens in the *freeze,* it gets stuck in the body, and it needs your active participation to move it from the past and incorporate it into your current awareness. Otherwise, it can become something that 'just happens to you,' when you're triggered. Our natural response to *perceived* threat is to fight, flight, and/or freeze. This response is so automatic, and so fast, that not much thinking happens. When the brain tells the body it's in danger of being seriously hurt or destroyed, the body simply gets to work protecting itself. Blood is redistributed, senses are heightened, unnecessary bodily functions are halted, and if necessary, a death-like state (freeze) is employed—all in the attempt to survive. Once the assessment is made, and the fight, flight, freeze series is activated, the body begins recording every aspect of the experience on a cellular level. Even in the freeze state, the amygdala is recording in detail what is happening to your body while you're unconscious or 'out'. Once you regain consciousness, the traumatic event must be address and organized. If not, the body will start to behave as if it has been infected by a foreign entity.

If we can separate the emotional and cognitive attachments from a traumatic event momentarily, meaning think about what happened without feeling or judging the information. If we can manage this for a short time, it becomes a simple exchange of information. So, the brain receives information and communicates it to the body, the body responds and sends information back; again, the brain sends updated information and the body again responds. However, when experiencing the freeze response to an event, the body is offline and cannot respond to the information being sent by the brain and is unable to send information back. This information breakdown and corresponding overload, causes the brain and body to short circuit. In order for the brain and body to get back online and reestablish an effective communication flow, the unprocessed (frozen) information must be organized and processed to enable the flow of communication. But without debugging or defragging the pieces of information, the brain and body will behave like a virus has taken over, resulting in *disorder.*

So, this backlog of unprocessed, mental, emotional, physical and psychological information is the disorder in all psychological disorders. That a traumatic event occurred in a baby, young child, teenager, young adult or middle-aged person does not matters. What matters is if, and how, it has been addressed. There is only healed or unhealed trauma—period. Again, the tendency to find fault, point fingers and defend (judgment, guilt and shame), will only serve to delay or prevent healing. Not all trauma is cause by intentional harm, AND accidental punches still hurt. So, without judgement, guilt and shame, what any trauma needs is the opportunity and support to heal. And it will; much like any other wound. What makes psychological trauma different is the absence of visible physical damage. We can't see the scrapes, scratches, cuts, punctures and breaks left on the heart, and mind, following the loss of a job, pet, house, friend, family member, comrade, battle buddy, hometown, spouse or anything else of value. This can be especially true for young children, who often have no say in how life happens to them. For example, frequent relocations, divorces, joblessness, homelessness, and other adult situations, have significant and lasting effects on children into adulthood. Car crashes and surgeries (major or minor) can also be quite traumatizing for children, and left unattended, can affect the kind of adults they become.

Countless studies have shown the lasting effects of childhood trauma on adulthood. What's difficult, is trying to name the cause without judgment, guilt and shame. Often, parents and caregivers are so preoccupied with their own survival, they can miss how some of their choices might have unintentionally harmful consequences for their children. I've worked with families in community mental health, where I have witness multigenerational trauma survivors. I've also worked with affluent families with multigenerational traumas. In both cases it is the walls of judgment, guilt and shame that prevents or delays healing. Trauma doesn't care how much, or how little, money or education you have. It waits to be validated, and it has a life time to wait. Losing a loved one, a friend, a home or some other significant thing, hurts. That loss must be validated and healed or there will be an indefinite space where the lost thing once was. Simply explaining the loss and ways to reconcile it will go a long way in helping the healing process along. No; we cannot bring anyone back from the dead; but, we can find ways to celebrate their life and have mementoes to help. Unlike adults, children haven't learned to lie and deny their feelings. This can be very uncomfortable for a wounded parent or caregiver to recognized, when they're often drowning in their own pain, grief and loss. The intent of this revelation, is to remind us that because there is no expiration date for trauma, addressing the loss as soon as possible is crucial. Unprocessed trauma will sit as frozen as the day it occurred, until it is triggered unintentionally, or finally acknowledged and validated. Until a traumatic event is addressed, survivors can experience debilitating emotional, psychological and physiological symptoms, diseases, and disorders, throughout their lives. Symptoms can range from persistent irritability, anger, sadness, anxiety and depression, to headaches, stomach aches, indigestion, diabetes, hypertension, and heart disease. These symptoms can, and often do, appear following traumas that are mistakenly regarded as, 'no big deal', or 'just part of life.'

To the individual experiencing the significant loss, there is a distinct mark in the time of life before, and after, a traumatic event. It is remarkable how clients can pinpoint, with relative accuracy, the moment their sense of safety, trust and wholeness, was lost. I usually ask clients, if they know their anniversaries; or I'll ask if they remember the last time they felt safe and happy. The answers to these questions can vary from, never, five years old, ten years old, a specific month, or a specific time of year. Either way, the body knows, and remembers! The body reacts with uncanny predictability around the anniversary, relating to the trauma. For example, many survivors will start to feel irritable, agitated, sad, anxious, angry, withdrawn, and, or defensive, around the anniversary of a significant loss. They have a recurring body pain or sickness around the same time each year. There's usually a general feeling of uneasiness, that can't be explained until you acknowledge its source. For survivors, and caregivers, this can be a scary and frustrating time. Because it seems to come on so suddenly, it can feel like your life is being hijacked.

I often hear, "I just feel angry all the time for no reason, or "I just feel really sad for no reason." Many clients will say "my depression is acting up again," or "my anxiety is off the charts again," or "I thought I was getting better but I feel like I'm exactly where I started." These are good indicators that the survivor is in an anniversary cycle. Caregivers will say, "what happened? I thought we were making progress," or "I thought we were doing so well," or "I thought he, or she, was getting over it." Unaddressed, anniversaries can derail the healing progress for survivors and loved ones. Anniversary time usually last about a six weeks, which is long enough for the wounded part of you to do some serious damage; to you, your relationships and environment. Because trauma has no expiration date, it doesn't lose its intensity, or power over the victim; until it is intentionally addressed and healed, it waits. This means that without your attention, intention and validation, it bleeds.

There is no expiration date, and there is no 'it just happens.' Everything the body does, it does for a reason. Every sensation and every emotion, is a message. The body is an intricately, intelligently designed machine, with the ability to heal itself, given the necessary attention, time and support—love. Doctors don't heal, they facilitate the conditions necessary for the body to heal. The same is true for therapists, counselors, family and friends. We don't heal the trauma survivors, we support, listen and love them, and each other, through the darkness and pain of psychological trauma. But it is the survivor who must start the healing process. It is the survivor who must give himself, or herself, permission to heal. It is the survivor who must tell someone there is a wound to be healed or listen and acknowledge the wound when someone points it out.

Usually, once the trauma anniversary is acknowledged, symptoms are reduced. I often suggest an active and conscious memorial event for the survivor, to both mourn and commemorate surviving the trauma. It is important for trauma survivors to reclaim this moment of powerlessness. This is not a new concept. It's why we have countless memorials and cemeteries. They are conscious and tangible places that provide a way to remember and acknowledge surviving a horrible loss.

On the following pages you are invited to try remembering and write down the last time you felt safe and happy. If you have a therapist or counselor, this information can help move your treatment forward. These recollections may be intensely personal and, or, painful. So, use your best judgment when, or if, you choose to share your traumas. I strongly suggest sharing with a professional first and getting guidance on who else to share with. Depending on the trauma history, trust may have been violated in very intimate ways; which can severely damage the ability to perceive healthy boundaries. Be safe. Think about and write down the first time you felt like you could no longer trust yourself, a family member, a partner, a friend, an employer, or GOD (for many trauma survivors a loss of faith in a higher power is a reality). Do you know your trauma anniversaries? It does not have to be the exact date of the loss; the time of year, or your age at the time, is sufficient. Write down your anniversaries and share them with a trusted person. It could be helpful to start logging your mood patterns as well. Again, there are no wrong answers. This is an invitation not a demand. As a survivor or caregiver, these notes can be extremely helpful in understanding the extreme mood swings that accompany many psychological disorders. Your journey, your pace. When ready, do this in a nonjudgmental way.

Notes

Notes

Notes

YOU MUST DECIDE TO LEAVE THE POSTTRAUMATIC CAVE

This revelation is a call to physical action and somewhat more concrete a concept than the first three. The cave feels safe. Thick walls, small windows, barricades and alarms, one-way visibility, secluded and most of all yours alone. This cave can be a physical structure such as a house, apartment or cabin in the woods, or it can be a mental and emotional escape that protects you from would-be intruders, friends or lovers. In your cave, everything is predictable, safe and in order. Only a select few know it exists, where it is, or how to get there, and absolutely no one can visit without your prior notice and permission. In this place, there is no chance of surprise or betrayal (two major ingredients of a traumatic event). In this place, you survive. You know every sound, smell, taste, touch and feel of it. Everything has its place. You have your routine, as well as extensive plans for any deviations from that routine. No surprises! Well done. This is existing, but this is not living.

Living is a choice and it is different from simply surviving. Given how hard you have worked to create and maintain such a secure, safe and secret place, no one is coming to you. You must take the first step. And while there is something to be said for alone-time and self-reflection, you must leave your cave, if you want optimal healing from your trauma(s). You must find a way to reconnect. Again, *you weren't traumatized alone, and you won't heal alone.* The cave is made for and by the warrior. Warriors by design are lone survivors, self-reliant and independent. They interact with others only as it relates to a specific need, goal or mission. Every move and interaction is calculated and re-planned—no surprises. Socially, interactive people live in open, welcoming dwellings that are inviting. They live in a way that is more trusting, flexible and tolerant. Leaving your cave and choosing to live again requires trust, flexibility and tolerance— and most of all, courage. This means having a reasonable sense of self, and a sense of collaboration with your warrior self. Trusting yourself is the most important requirement—as this puts your warrior at ease. Knowing your triggers, knowing your body and knowing your emotions is critical as you go out into the world. Being aware of how your new (posttraumatic) mind and body works will make it easier to identify and communicate your needs. Knowing what sounds, sights, smells, touches and tastes you like and dislike, will help you engage in new relationships. Leaving your cave and reconnecting to others, is like giving birth to the new you. It is stepping out of the darkness and into the light. In many ways, the cave is like a womb; in that it is safe and protective. Your cave, like a womb, is dark, cozy, supportive and nurturing. And like all wombs, it can't hold you forever. All living things grow, transform and expand, and you are no exception. Time spent in the cave has its purpose posttraumatically. It allows you to stabilize, strengthen and become self-aware. And then it's time to present the new you to family, friends and community. Initially, yes; it can feel uncomfortable, scary, bright, loud, harsh, unpredictable, cold and even dangerous. All of this can be used as justification to 'just stay put.' I've had many survivors tell me, "I have all I need in my place." And being the kind of healer that I am, I respond with, 'so how do you explain the feelings of constant sadness, loneliness, fear and worry?' Most often I hear, "I don't know, but I'm ok." Other times I hear "I guess you got a point." The point is, we are social being, and we NEED to connect with others in order to feel whole—in order to recover and be healed.

The need for the cave is valid. Time to self-assess, time to lick your wounds or time to organize your thoughts and feelings. And because we were created in connection with another and was wounded in connection with another, we must heal in connection with another. It's that simple, and that complicated. Initially, we are not aware of our connection to the woman carrying us in her body; yet we are physically connected to her. We may not be consciously aware of our connection to whomever or whatever traumatized us, yet we will always feel a connection to it. And we may not yet know the person who will be the connecting bridge from our darkness back to life; yet he or she will show up when we reach for them. So, time in the posttraumatic cave can be part of your healing journey, but it should not be the eternal resting stop. If you haven't consciously done so, use the time in your cave to incubate, germinate and sprout the new you. Learn the difference between you and your warrior self. Foster, support and protect this new version of yourself, AND bring it out into the light and let it be loved, nurtured and supported by others. Once you've gotten an idea of your basic needs, leave the cave and introduce the new You to old friends, family members and community. Again, much like a new baby, slow and gradual introductions and interactions are highly recommended. Overstimulation of any new (baby, puppy, plant or you) living thing, can cause significant setbacks. Knowing who you really are, how you really feel and what you really want, is all that matters—as this can encourage you to interact and respond in socially appropriate ways. Making others' needs and wants more important than your own can activate a sense of injustice in the long run—potentially activating your warrior self. Expressing your wants and needs, as well as learning and respecting the needs and wants of those in your life, will help to achieve the life you want. Your warrior's purpose is to protect you. A warrior's desire is to win! So, give him or her challenges that will enhance life for the both of you.

We are social beings and need relationship to truly live full lives. Everything we are, is in relation to someone else—parent/child, husband/wife, intimate partners, student/teacher, boss/employee, merchant/customer, doctor/patient, warrior/civilian, firefighter/resident, waiter/patron, friends, enemies and so on. We are a species that is so interconnected, that if not touched as babies, will die. And countless studies show the importance of physical touch to emotional and psychological wellbeing throughout our lives. Intimate partners, spouses, friends, siblings; even wolves, bears, lions, elephants and whales need physical touch. There is a chemical, emotional and psychological response that supports and enhances healing and wellbeing that is activated with touch. While medications can help with chemical signals in the body, they cannot negate the need for social and emotional interaction.

There are countless scientific studies showing the importance of human relationships. These studies indicate that simply being in the room with another human being can affect your mental and emotional state. These studies also indicate that isolation is the most extreme form of punishment for a human. Regardless of how callus a person seems, isolation has the ability to 'break' them. Hence the use of solitary confinement in prisons to modify behaviors. Prolonged isolation is quite literally torture for a human being. On the other hand, it has been proven that we hurt less, and heal faster, with a supportive person nearby. Hospitals, hospices, orphanages, prisons or any place that house people, have programs that encourage and support visitors for residence. Even trauma survivors who have been victims of human-to human violations improved with the presence and, or interaction of other helpful and supportive people.

Many survivors will say "I don't need anyone," "I can make it on my own," "you can't trust anyone," "everybody lies," "everybody leaves" or "I'm better off alone." Well, they say admitting you have a problem is the first step to fixing it. And if we weren't social beings, there would be no problem with the above ways of thinking and being. We could all just go on surviving. Except that we ARE social beings and the fundamental thing needed in a social relationship is trust—the very thing that was BROKEN during the traumatic event. There is no such thing as an independent person. It's a lie we tell ourselves to numb the pain and feel better. No one makes it alone—no one! Business men need customers, banks need customers, doctors need patients, builders need home buyers, children need parents, friends need friends and lone survivors need food and supplies and so, need relationships that will facilitate the acquisition of those goods and services. No one makes it alone indefinitely; no one. You may have survived your traumatic experience alone, but you were not traumatized alone. Something or someone took away your sense of safety, and trust, in the world. And getting it back will require at least two souls, one being yours.

Trauma is about the loss of a relationship. A relationship between you and what was lost, a person, your identity, your job, your status, your family, your comrades, your values, your innocence or your faith. Something that was important to you was lost. This loss changed you forever. There is an empty space left inside of us after every traumatic event. And everything we do posttraumatically, is an attempt to fill that space. It can look different depending on who and what is available to meet this goal. From a trauma perspective, all that matters is ending the pain and filling the void. We just want to feel safe and in control again. Some survivors will form relationships with alcohol, drugs, work, gambling, school, sex, crises or an alternate reality. These relationships that were intended to help, can become addictions used to escape the pain and emptiness. And while they may be maladaptive, many survivors rationalize that, 'at least this can't betray me,' or 'at least I know what to expect' or 'at least I'm in control.' Unlike trusting a person; turning to alcohol, drugs, gambling, school, sex, work or crisis, gives survivors a sense of being in control. There's the belief that the addictive or compulsive behavior is predictable, dependable and under your control. That is, until the substance or activity is controlling the survivor. Many survivors find themselves, preoccupied with their next drink, next smoke, next fix, next presentation, next achievement, next assignment, next win, next trick or next high; all of which end up creating an entirely new set of problems. Ironically, problems that will require a relationship with other people to solve. Every addictions treatment program has built into it, some form of relationship with another person (a sponsor, a mentor, a battle buddy). These relationships require your willingness to relate, to connect, to reengage with people, the world and yourself.

So, the choice to leave the safety of your posttraumatic cave can be life changing for you and everyone you meet. Trauma is a disgusting surprise and it violates everything that made you *you*. So, the decision to live again, means learning to be a new you—a better, stronger and wiser version of yourself. The decision to leave the cave means trusting again. First you must learn to trust yourself. Believe you have what it takes to not only survive but live again. Giving unconditional love to this new you can be difficult when voices of judgement, guilt and shame fill your head. Leaving the cave provides opportunities to hear other voices, and points of view. It allows you to witness actions to the contrary of the negative stories of the internal warden and prisoner that may have become your 'normal' narrative.

Because trauma happens in the freeze, in the part of us

that is beyond words, beyond comprehension, beyond belief and beyond our sense of reality, we feel lost. Unaccompanied, trauma survivors can become consumed by and within this loss. So being willing to find yourself posttraumatically, is about feeling around in the darkness for the light switch. It means digging around in the pile of crap for the value, the meaning, the treasure that is you. You are not what happened to you. A hundred-dollar bill covered in shit, is still worth one-hundred dollars! I promise you, you are worth much more than one-hundred dollars!! The new you, is just that—new. The posttraumatic darkness can be both scary and comforting. It's scary initially for the newly traumatized; but can become comforting for those who have been there for too long. The cave has become their home and leaving has become more of a struggle. The longer we're in the darkness without support or guidance out, the more alone and callus we can become. And the more painful and difficult stepping into the light can feel. Getting support and confirmation that you're alive and have something to live for is paramount.

Isolation and avoidance are double edged swords. On one hand, you feel safe and protected. On the other hand, you feel uneasy and alone. There is no one to measure your progress or regress. Trauma survivors don't typically know their behaviors have changed posttraumatically. The body automatically adjusts and behaves in ways to compensate to make itself feel 'normal.' The body will compensate for a weaker limb by over using the strong one, a strong eye will automatically adjust vision to compensate for the weaker eye. Behaviorally, we instinctively avoid triggers related to the traumatic event, to feel safe. Without realizing it, we'll start avoiding left turns or specific streets after a car crash, drink alcohol to help with sleep, use cocaine to wake up or stay on schedule, work countless hours to avoid being at home alone or initiate sex to avoid feeling victimized. A diagnosis, or label, usually only comes when someone else is affected, or when work performance or school work is being compromised. Then bosses, teachers, coworkers, family members or friend start to comment on your behaviors since 'the accident,' or 'the thing.' In fact, part of the diagnostic process is to question the length of time you have had certain behaviors, and if they have interfered with 'normal' daily activities. Usually a spouse, family member, friend or coworker will comment that 'you've changed, or something's different about you.' Isolation and avoidance are such powerful coping strategies that survivors can go for years without a diagnosis and without support, especially if there are no witnesses to notice any changes or unusual behaviors. Vietnam veterans are an excellent example of this. Many Vietnam veterans have been able to avoid, or delay, a PTSD diagnosis until they've reached retirement age, and can no longer use work to outrun or avoid the pain of their 40 plus year-old war wounds. Many have long histories of broken families, divorces and sporadic employment (often complements of the warrior part of themselves). It's not until the trauma survivor (with or without military experience), connects with someone else who is close enough, long enough, to remind them, or show them, the psychological and emotional wounds, and how they have bled (patterns of emotional/psychological destruction) all over the life they want to have. Trauma survivors are often so numb to the psychological and emotional needs of relationships. Often, they don't make the connection between their behaviors and their effects on the relationship, until it's too late. Someone might say, 'why don't you drive anymore,' 'why don't you live closer to your family,' or 'why don't you leave the house after dark' or 'why don't you talk to that person anymore...?' In the safety of the cave there is no way to assess progress or regress posttraumatically, without a relationship.

If avoidance and isolation is a double-edged sword, then falling in love can feel like a doubled-edged, jagged machete.

To a wounded heart, the intimacy and intensity of emotional closeness and vulnerability, can be disorienting. The choice to leave your cave invites the chance that someone will meet you, and like you. For better or worse, you are not your trauma. There is an amazing person under that pile of shit that is the trauma response (and its consequences). The choice to leave the cave, interact, reconnect and socialize, brings with it the exposure of all that you are. As you start to heal, and find yourself, you will attract people. You will not only attract healers and supporters. You will attract friends and potential mates. This is where trauma survivors can get derailed in their efforts to heal, because we only have one heart, and one brain. We have one heart that feels and remembers every experience; every hurt, every joy, every betrayal, every loss, every triumph. And since there is no delete button, every emotion leaves a mark on the heart. And we have one brain that records and calculates every event; every date, every break-up, every battle, every commitment, every violation, every collaboration, every asset and liability, is recorded and filed away in the brain. This endless recording of emotional and psychological information makes for an expansive database in our bodies, that is designed to keep us safe. No delete button means that our history can become justification for the cave, and the defensive behaviors warriors use against potential future offenders (real or imagined). Letting someone get close enough to love you, touch you, open old files of painful information, and expose old vulnerabilities, means running the risk of losing and being hurt again. And because we only have one heart, and one brain, intimate relationships are especially challenging when the heart and mind have been wounded.

Falling in love posttraumatically, can feel like salt on an open wound. Who wants that, right? Funny thing about salt water, it cleanses, purifies and heals wounds. Like all things, moderation, and method, matters. Getting to know yourself is the first step to any meaningful relationship, from friends, coworkers, comrades, to lovers. Knowing who you are, and how you show up in relationships, is crucial to the success of that relationship. Falling in love is different from any other relationship, primarily because it is unplanned; hence the word 'falling.' And given that trauma survivors don't typically do well with surprises, being in an intimate relationship can be very disruptive to the recovery process. This disruption will certainly feel like a threat to your warrior self. And in a misguided attempt to keep you 'safe,' he or she *will* attempt to terminate this relationship. It takes a level head, and a courageous, understanding, and forgiving heart to communicate through this new, and messy, development. People make mistakes, and the closer the person is to you, emotionally, the bigger the mistake will feel. Slow and steady. Constantly communicating feelings and intent, as often as possible, or as often as is necessary to feel safe will go a long way is moving the relationship forward. As with all things, ***less is best, when you are stressed.*** I think the cowboy was right when he said, 'speak slow and low.' While this approach can be applied in many cases, it is especially helpful when attempting to communicate with an emotional trauma survivor. And it just doesn't get any more emotional than falling in love, and out of control (control being the one thing trauma survivors live for).

Love is a loaded word, to say the least. It is the ultimate four-letter-word! It's what the wounded person both craves and fears. Love heals us, defends us, protect us, shelters us and gives us purpose. Love is the reason we do anything, and the absence of love is why we do everything else. Think about it. Every productive thing you do, you do because you love something or someone, and every destructive thing you do, you do because of the painful void where love once was. We tend to confuse loving something or someone with possessing it or them. Falling in love can have negative connotation. It can feel like the loss of something—yourself, your freedom or control. And from a wounded point of view, this feels very true. But as I stated earlier, while the state of 'falling in love' can feel terrifying, it's being experienced through the stock pile of painful trauma memories. We are not born afraid of anything. We are born loving, trusting, giving, forgiving, receptive, sensitive, free and curious. This is our natural state. We mutate into angry, defensive, suspicious, fearful, vengeful, callused, isolated, withdrawn and imprisoned survivors, as we endure countless traumas that are left unacknowledged, unresolved and unhealed.

I am not particularly proud of the person I was in my teens and twenties. I was oblivious to the needs of people around me. I was so far from myself and consequently detached from the needs of others. I was careless and reckless. I was good at putting on the show, but every show ends, and I would move on with little, if any, thought about the affect I'd had on the other person. Usually, I'd let the relationship end under the guise of haven been wronged by the other person. I convinced myself that they had betrayed or neglected me in some way. Thus, justifying the inevitable end. I don't need you, and you don't need me, was my unspoken mantra. It wasn't until my second divorce, several attempts at reconciliation and the scolding of my daughter about never giving anyone a real chance, that I started to take an active account of my behavior in personal relationships. I took a along break (several years) to consciously recount my steps and missteps. I started looking at the patterns and noticed how I had been 'loving guarded.' My daughter was right. I never gave anyone a chance, that included myself. There was no real chance to love or be loved, and consequently, no chance of being hurt, abandoned or surprised. I was under control and out of my mind. But, I wanted more. Not yet for me, but for my children. I wanted them to know love, freedom, friendship, companionship, intimacy and trust. And since kids do what we do, and not what we say, I knew I had to start with me. So, I started working on my own cave. Being somewhat of a nomad, mine was an emotional and psychological cave. I moved a lot, and made 'friends' everywhere I went, and then moved again. But love calls us out. It makes us want more, to be more, to have more, to do more. Love is a full-time job—and this is just self-love. Cleaning up my mental cave meant really looking at myself and how I showed up. It meant caring for and falling in love with me! I've come to realize that love is freedom, and freedom is not free! It costs time, energy and courage! I'll say that again, freedom is not free; it costs time, energy and courage. The courage to truly look at, and see, yourself, is humbling. To look, and see, the wounds, the scars, the monster and the warrior, takes guts. To truly see the loneliness, the pain, the fear; and keep looking until you see the victim, the survivor, the prince, the princess, the jewel.

WE are so much more than our losses. WE are so much more than our traumas. WE just have to remember who we ARE. Feel around in the darkness and have the courage to step out of our caves and into love. Yes, I said step into love. Feel free to fall, but I've learned that that's usually intense infatuation, and we typically jump out of it as quickly as we fell in. Real love, real healing, real freedom takes conscious effort. It takes time. It takes energy. It takes courage. You can choose to dab the saltwater on the wound to heal the it, or plunge in, and jump out running. Love is the healing potion that we all crave, and many fear. Ironically, the more we crave it, the more we fear it. We fear it because it strips us of all armor. Love is shameless that way. It's fearless and reckless; it doesn't care about getting hurt because it can't be hurt. Love dares us to try and try again. It makes us brave. It makes us vulnerable. Most, if not all, warriors equate vulnerability with weakness. But love is too bold and shameless to care. It just is. Think about a one-year old baby. They are shameless, bold, trusting, happy and free. That's what love is. That all gets distorted when we are traumatized. But again, there's no delete button; so, it's still in there. The memories of loving and being loved, shamelessly, are there; just buried. I've learned that it starts with you, where you are; in your cave. Love is an inside job that can become a healing fountain that can heal others.

Leaving your cave and opening to the possibility of letting someone in, can be terrifying. You've invested a lot of your time, and energy building this cave. You've spent days, weeks, months and years trying to create a safe fortress. Friends, coworkers, and even family members have limited, if any, access to this fortress. But being in an intimate relationship, means letting someone get close enough to see, and touch, things and places of deep meaning and value. Being in love not only means leaving your cave; it also means letting someone else into your cave. It means showing and risking your most treasured, guarded and ugliest secrets. It means exposing your soft, vulnerable, amazing, sensitive, scary, ferocious, sad, passive, anxious and aggressive parts—it means showing someone *all* of who you really are. And trusting them to stay. But more importantly, trusting yourself to keep living if, and when, they leave. Because everybody leaves at some point. Be it by way of death, when an old spouse of 70+ years passes away, or the death of the relationship itself. All things change, and end, in one form or another. A new job, a new baby, and sick friend or family member can all change a relationship. These events can force a relationship to change, adapt or end. When trauma survivors are forced to change unexpectedly, or drastically, they can feel overwhelmed, abandoned or betrayed. These feeling will certainly get the warrior's attention. Knowing and loving yourself will prevent unnecessary harm to yourself, the other person and the relationships.

Falling in love can feel like heaven and hell all at once. Depending on where you are on your healing journey. An intimate relationship can propel you forward or pull you backward. Self-awareness and self-love is crucial! Experiences of love, fear, joy, anger and sadness all come to pass. Nothing stays. Nothing lasts forever. The best orgasm will end. The worst pain will end. The meaning we give to the person, or event, that is ending, or changing, will determines the effect the loss, or change, has on us. The best job, the best partner, the worse job or the worse partner—subjective to you and your interpretation of it; will change or end. For better or worse, you get to decide. The willingness to be the next best version of yourself is a lifelong commitment. It is the willingness to dare to live. Knowing things will change, and you along with them, makes the journey worth the effort. Even in the safety of your cave, you experience changes. As you adjust to how your body changes, or how, where, or when you get supplies to restock your cave. All things change. That we can share these changes with someone else, makes life worth living, celebrating, mourning, anticipating and talking about.

What are the benefits to staying isolated in your cave? What are the risks of leaving your cave? What are the potential benefits to leaving your cave or inviting someone else in? Can you recognize that you have created a cave since your traumatic event(s)?

Pause.

Think about how your cave has served you. Think about how your need to feel safe has affected your connections with other people in your life. Are there friends and loved ones who have been dismissed or held at a distance? On the following pages, you are invited to write any thoughts and answers to these questions. As always, there are no wrong answers. Try to identify people and places that have overwhelmed you in such a way that your cave has become either reinforced or less of a necessity.

Notes

Notes

YOU ARE THE ONLY REASON
TO TRY ENDLESSLY

This revelation can sound daunting and farfetched. Endlessly!? Really?! Yes. For as long as you're alive you are changing, and as long as you are changing, you have a choice in how you change. Surviving or existing are possible choices, and different from living. Life is filled with inherent risk, mostly the risk of failure or loss. It is unavoidable. You will lose something, and you will gain something as well. For every loss, there is a gain. Pleasure is not without pain. Light is not without dark. Courage is not without fear. Peace is not without conflict. To know and have one, is to appreciate the other. Losing your old self, your old life and your innocence can be devastating. Losing your sense of self can make you wish for death. In many ways, you did die; and yet here you are reading this book. Perhaps searching for meaning. Perhaps searching for a way to the new you. Or maybe you're looking for a reason to say, 'I've tried, and now I'm done.' Whatever the case, you are here because of a significant loss; looking for a reason. You are that reason. And I am sorry for your pain. I am also celebrating your courage. I celebrate your courageous effort to heal what has been broken and restore what was lost (your sense of self). I have learned that the next best version of ourselves is just on the other side of every experience; if we choose to step into it. You survived hell and now have a choice to make. Live, or wait to die.

Because trauma is about the complete loss of control, over yourself and your environment, the posttraumatic life becomes a series of extreme choices that are attempts to regain control and prevent that traumatic event from ever happening again. Trauma is a terrifying, horrifying surprise that leaves you feeling helpless and hopeless. A trauma survivor's life is about *never* getting caught off guard again. The extreme choices designed to help us cope with the pain and loss, become labels like: control freak, alcoholic, workaholic, drug addict, depressed, anxious, defiant, angry, oppositional, withdrawn, isolated, bipolar, borderline, schizophrenic, lazy, bitch, asshole, doormat, slut, antisocial, and on and on. The choice to stay stuck is a coping strategy. However maladaptive it may be—it is a way of trying to stay 'safe.' In this stuck place, there is the safety of knowing what to expect, however horrible or painful—at least there are no surprises. And in doing so, we stay stuck in the cycle of judgment, guilt and shame. But just on the other side of this choice, is the next best you—the reason. The You that survived hell. The You that chose to live. The You that fought and won! The only person in the universe that can be you. This You, waits to be discovered and expressed.

Many trauma survivors will say 'why bother trying.' And to them I say, because you're still here. Try because you cared enough about something or someone to survive. Something inside of you chose to survive a horrifying, terrifying event that left you, for a time, feeling helpless and hopeless. You survived!! The interesting thing about surviving a traumatic event is, the person you were, before the event, doesn't know that you're alive. He or she is 'frozen' in that moment of terror. In a way, the traumatic event is sandwiched between the *new* you (who survived) and the *old* you (who froze waiting to die). In many ways, the 'disorder' is the static, the disconnection or broken communication, between you and your old self. You try to get over it, around it or past it, but the only way is through the wall that is the traumatic event. And get to the next best version of yourself.

Many times, I hear people say, "I just need to get over it, or I should just get past it." But much like a fuse that has been damaged by a surge of electricity, your internal communication system has been 'blown.' Trauma has the same effect on the body as a surge of an electrical current. You have been physiologically rewired. Finding yourself posttraumatically, is much like an electrician exploring the wiring of a house. This person must find the source of the surge (the traumatic event), and the extent of the damage (what was lost) before attempting any repairs. You wouldn't expect an electrician to repair the blown fuse by just walking over the roof of the house, or walking past, or around the house? No, you expect them to come inside, perform an assessment, an evaluation, an investigation, and explain the findings, before any work is done. Finding and repairing yourself requires at least the same kind of attention and exploration. The repair work can be delayed, avoided and denied; but if you want full recovery of the flow of electricity in the house, or satisfying emotional/psychological communication in your body and life, the work must be done. Otherwise, there will always be a part of the house— of you, that is disconnected and out of order. Unaddressed, there will always be dark areas unavailable for use in your house and life.

So, trauma is unprocessed or unaddressed emotional/psychological damage. In fact, thanks to researchers and trauma experts like Bessel van der Kolk, Dan Siegel, Daniel Amen and Peter Levine, we know this to be true. Trauma is unprocessed information that is trapped in various parts of the body. Evidence of the effects of emotional and psychological trauma to the brain can be seen using PET (positron emission tomography) or SPECT (single photon emission computed tomography). With this information, we can start to plan and calculate how and when to treat and support trauma survivors. Knowing and understanding that you have been quite literally changed by the event on a physical level, should give you permission to heal. While we still cannot see meaning or value, we can see the damage caused when something meaningful and valued is lost. I am hopeful that with continued work of experts in the field of mind and brain health, we will continue to collect the evidence needed to give ourselves permission to move toward the next best version of ourselves.

Once we've looked at the source or cause (the traumatic event), and the extent of the damage, physical, emotional and psychological (what was lost), we can start to budget for the repairs. We can research treatment options, modalities and strategies. We can now assess for support options and recovery planning. Who do we trust to support us through the healing process; friends, family, professionals, peers? Do we need individual, family or group therapy? Should we find a specific kind of therapy, as specialist or will a friend, or family member, be enough? We must look under the hood, so to speak before making any decisions about repair and recovery. Whatever you choose, feeling safe and supported is the most important thing.

I like the analogy of a vehicle when discussing emotional and psychological issues. In general, people tend to take better care of their vehicles than they do themselves. We get regular oil changes, tire replacements, breaks, tune ups. Some people even name their vehicles or give them a gender. After a crash, we're on the phone with the insurance company, getting estimates, planning repairs and looking forward to the new version of our damaged car. But when it comes to self-maintenance, self-care or self-repair following a traumatic experience (an emotional, psychological crash), we're willing to drive on the spare tire, skip the oil change, ignore the check engine light, ignore the broken windows. It's as if self-care isn't as important. It's as if psychological and emotional damage doesn't matter. It's as if there's too much to lose by getting the work done. Much like a neglected vehicle, eventually we break down. You only get so many warning lights before the engine blows, breaks give out or the tire pops. In most cases, a good mechanic can fix all of this, but sometimes we need an entirely new car. In a similar way, you only get so many warnings before depression, anxiety, aggression, addiction or suicidal/homicidal ideations take over. Before long, we lose friends, family members, the job, the partner, the house, and in some instances, life. Where vehicles and people differ in this example, is the benefit/cost analysis. There's no way to put a cost on psychological and emotional damage. What is taken during a traumatic event is priceless. What is lost during a traumatic event is beyond words. It's an individualized value, with individualized meaning. We can shop around for auto parts and repair estimates. We cannot shop around for psychological and emotional parts and repair estimates. This inability to put concrete value on what was lost can add to the damage and prolong healing. The inability to assign meaning or understanding to what was lost, can make us feel worthless and hopelessness. The inability to assign a value, can leave us feeling overwhelmed, and asking why bother. The inability to standardize the trauma response can leave trauma survivors feeling lost and neglected. Because trauma is subjective, we only have a generalized description, with vague explanations and questionable treatment strategies.

There is no one size fits all. You are the only you. No one knows what it's like to be you. No one can ever know what it's like to be you. But what we can do is be compassionate, supportive and nonjudgmental. We know that given a real opportunity, all living things heal. Given support and compassion all living things will heal. Without judgment, guilt or shame; love heals. Finding the next best version of yourself, requires self-love, self-compassion. If you don't love yourself, you won't allow anyone else to love you. If you don't like yourself, you won't believe that anyone else likes you. You are the gatekeeper. You choose to believe your current circumstance, and what you believe will either open the gate, or keep it locked. The next best version of yourself is just outside that gate. If you decide that it is safer to stay put or step out into the next version of yourself; you are right. The choice to search for the newest version of ourselves, starts with one small choice; the choice to believe that there is such a person. We must first believe that who we are right now, in this moment, has all that we need to be better, stronger, wiser and happier versions of ourselves. This means the choice to believe that you are worth getting out of bed for. You are worth brushing your teeth for. You are worth leaving the house for. You are worth the effort and courage it takes to try. All you have to lose is an old belief system that has held you hostage.

What you gain is a better awareness of who you are—if you're paying attention. Every choice has a cost, and your willingness to pay that cost will dictate the choices you make. The choice to leave the safety of your posttraumatic cave, means being willing to trust again. It means betting on you. You're betting that even if you fall, you can get back up, even if you lose you can start again, even if someone leaves you, you still have yourself, and with time, that becomes your most valuable asset; You. If you like yourself, and know yourself, you will never be alone because you will attract people who like you, and want to know you, and be around you. Every break up, every firing, every loss has buried inside of it the next best version of you. Just as every acorn has an oak tree inside, and every apple seed has an apple tree in side, and every caterpillar has a butterfly inside, every ending as you know it, has the next best version of you inside. You are the only you there has ever been, or will ever be. No one else can do you like you. No one else can love, hate, fear, heal, teach, dance, write, sign, draw, laugh or cry like you—no one!

Trusting yourself to find and be this next version of you, is the work of healing posttraumatically. Your environment will change constantly. People, jobs, family, friends, cars, houses and even body functions, will all come and go. Your ability, and willingness, to search for, and find, the next best version of yourself will move you through these changes with a renewed sense of purpose. And it depends solely on you. You are the one constant in your life. You were created to be the best possible expression of yourself. You are the only reason to try endlessly. I know this sounds selfish and it is; because if you don't take good care of yourself, who will take care of the things and people you care about? You can't give a ride with a broken-down car. You can't feed the hungry if you're passed out. There will always be someone who needs you—you. And if you don't answer that call, you won't be there for anyone else for very long. 'Put your own oxygen mask on first!' Otherwise, you and those you care about will be dead.

Regardless of your environment this does not change. Your experiences may slow you down or speed you up, but they cannot stop you unless you stop trying. We all ask the questions, 'what is my purpose,' 'why am I here,' or 'why did this happen to me?' The answers to these questions sit quietly inside of you; waiting to be discovered by you. We must be willing to dig through the shit to find the jewel. The jewel is you! The next best version of you. We must become miners of our own treasure. Yes, it can feel wrong, unfair, unjust and shitty! AND it's your pile of crap to do with what you choose. You can carry it around, showing it off to everyone you meet, telling the story of how you were crapped on, how heavy it is, how bad it smells, how bad it feels, how hard it is to live with such a big stinky load. Or you can try to bury it, hide it, deny it, minimize it and pretend like it doesn't exist, it never happened, and it's no big deal. Deny or complain, both are valid options, but at some point, something inside of you calls you back to your truth, your purpose.

This something is your true Self, and it demands order and justice. By justice, I mean the right to be seen, heard, believed and celebrated. The Right to Be what you were created to be. This Divine Right can be expressed in prison, in church, in an alley, in a mansion or in a war-torn country. Every living thing is given this Right, and along with it, the call to express it. And by order, I mean the cleaning and rearranging of life posttraumatically. Trauma always leaves a mess behind. Notice the labels that often follow a traumatic event—posttraumatic stress *disorder*, anxiety *disorder*, depressive *disorder*, bipolar *disorder* and so on. Trauma shatters our sense of wholeness; making it difficult to communicate and orient ourselves. There's a broken sense of time, space, emotion and sensation. Trauma survivors often communicate in broken sentences, with broken timelines, and mismatched emotional responses, and are consequently accused of lying and being stupid and crazy (by themselves and by others). The disorder and judgement that follows a traumatic event is the pile of crap that we carry around. We often show up with misguided attempts at restoring a sense of order and justice. There is no pill, there is no drink, there is no weapon, there is no prison, and there is no one, that can undo what was done! The internal healing work is ours alone to do. The growth, and recovery, is ours alone to do. We must be willing to do the healing work, if we want to live again. We must be willing to ask for, and receive, the support needed for posttraumatic healing. No one can heal us, only support and witness, with love and respect. Doctors don't heal the broken bone. They only provide the supportive conditions necessary for the bone to heal. Searching for, and finding, the next best version of yourself posttraumatically will take all the courage you have. Discovering, uncovering, seeking and finding are all action words meaning to look for. What we are looking for is the jewel, the purpose, the being, the reason. We are looking for the next best version of ourselves. This is the growing work, the healing work, that allows us to be the next best version of ourselves. It can be hard, AND it is not impossible. We just have to get out of our own way.

Human beings are the only living things that resist growth. As little babies, we do just fine. We reach out and grab the finger of any loving hand within reach. We trust instinctively, love and forgive unconditionally. For the first few years of life, there is a knowing, a wisdom, that allows for shameless, guiltless trust and forgiveness (ironically allowing for the most fertile time of human growth and learning). I learned about forgiveness from my daughter when she was two years old. She was bitten by a little boy in her daycare class and I was given an 'incident report.' I was furious to say the least. My beautiful baby had this huge bite mark on her gorgeous little cheek, and I wanted blood. I wanted 'justice'! I questioned the teacher with the calm fury of a mother bear. She was polite and diplomatic as she explained that they could not release the name of the child, but that I could be assured that the proper steps were taken to insure my daughter's safety. I was not happy nor satisfied with her little spiel. On the way home, I questioned my little two-year-old and over the span of that evening, and the next morning, I continued to question her. Trying to get the information I needed to exact my vengeance—not really sure what that would look like. But questioned and grilled I did, until finally I had a name. Over the next day or so the mark on her face became a dark green and purple bruise. I was beside myself; it took everything in me to control my emotions and my behaviors; especially when I saw my bruised Angelgirl playing with this little boy the very next day. I rushed over, grabbed my child, and said something to the effect of, what are you doing? we don't play with biters. And she 'matter of factly' responded with, "he said sorry and gave me a hug. We're friends now." I thought to myself, friends now!? Friends now! but the bruise is huge and still on your face!? Instant forgiveness, done, she's over it. She's back to her life and I'm holding this anger. The beauty and luxury of childhood is the ability and willingness to love and be loved unconditionally and unafraid.

The problems start as soon as we learn about judgement, guilt and shame—the barriers to healing and growth. Before we learn about judgement, guilt and shame, we forgive instantly and try repeatedly. As young children, we will try over and over and over until we learn, to feed ourselves, walk, run, clothe ourselves, read, write, and talk. Have you ever seen a baby try to eat spaghetti or green peas? It's adorable! The spaghetti falls off the spoon; the peas roll off the spoon; and still they try and try. Finally, they use their hands, but they get it done—they eat. No judgment, no guilt, no shame. They just do their best. The first five years are explosive for the human brain! So much is learned and then slows and slows and slows with increased judgement, guilt and shame. I was stuck in my judgment of that little boy who bit my daughter, and I wanted him to feel guilty and ashamed for what he did. I wanted him to feel what I felt when I saw my daughter's bruised face. But he didn't; he couldn't, he only saw his friend. And my daughter never spoke of it again. She forgave and moved on. But she knows the story, because for years I couldn't let it go.

I did eventually learn the lesson and continue to use it as a reminder that forgiveness takes nothing away, except the burden of judgement. Many people need the judgment to feel validated in their pain. So, we exact guilt and shame, hoping against hope that our pain will be realized by the offender. But it can never be. It can never be, because you're the only you, and you are the only one who feels it the way you feel it. Judgment feeds guilt and shame. Without judgement, there is no guilt to be ashamed of. Judgement allows for the angry energy needed to fuel the fight against the pain. Some might say the fight for justice. But what is justice? And how does it heal the pain of a traumatic loss? What is lost in trauma is beyond justice. Just as science cannot prove a theory, traumatic loss cannot be justified. Theories can only be disproven, and traumatic wounds can only be healed. There's not enough money, jail time or death, to heal or replace the loss of a loved one, a comrade, fellow warriors, a body part, or one's innocence. Only the courage of a newborn to reach out, love and trust, can heal what is lost in trauma.

If we lay down the judgment, there's only the pain of guilt and shame. And that's hard and can feel unbearable to live with. We resist the realization that growth is uncomfortable, necessary AND rewarding. The comfort, and familiarity, of anger, anxiety and sadness is a seductive trap. They are almost like a safety blanket. We get wrapped up in the anger, the anxiety and the depression. We give these labels power over our lives. I often hear, "I can't because my depression is back," or "I would but my anxiety won't let me," or "I can't trust my anger." It's as if we're married to the label and it has us trapped. This trap robs us of so much; because, there is also peace, love and joy available, when we step toward healing and away from judgment, guilt and shame. Laying down our armor, our blankets and our weapons posttraumatically, leaves us feeling vulnerable and naked. It also leaves us open to the possibility of recovery and discovery of our next best selves. Some of us get it as we get older and find the courage to heal and be healed. Others take longer to shed their defenses. The healing journey is as individualized as the traumatic experience itself. But what every trauma survivor has in common is a buried jewel waiting to be discovered, recovered and expressed. You are the reason to try again.

How are you different now, from who/what you were before your trauma(s)? Have you forgiven yourself for being too young, too weak, too naïve, too incapable of topping or preventing the trauma(s)? Have you forgiven your offender? Is forgiveness possible?

Pause.

What do you think, and how do you feel, about a 'new version of yourself'? Is there anything about you that you like? Is there anything about you that you liked before the trauma(s)? Can you remember who or what you wanted to be before your sense of peace and safety was taken? Can you remember ever feeling a sense of peace and safety? On the following pages, you are invited to explore old dreams you've had. What, when, and where do not matter. Be with your thoughts and feelings, allow your mind and heart to wander and search through the pile of crap, the prickly and dark forests of trauma and pain history. This search and rescue message might take a while, and that's okay. When you're ready, think, feel and search; write down your findings. What did you dream of becoming? How have those dreams changed? Do you have new dreams? Could be that you have no current or conscious dreams at this time, and that's ok too. All observations are valid and helpful on the healing journey. Knowing where you are is just as important as knowing where you want to go. So, allow the answers to come to you and write them down without judgement. Be a compassionate and patient excavator.

Notes

Notes

YOU MUST SHARE THE GIFT OF YOU, THERE'S A REASON YOU'RE STILL ALIVE

This revelation is a call to celebrate and expand the new posttraumatic you. Many people wander through life unaware and uninterested in why they are here. Trauma survivors are different. Posttraumatically, you become very interested in answering the questions, "why am I still here," "why did I survive and he, she or they didn't," "why didn't I die" "how am I still alive after" "what is my purpose...?" These are all common and valid questions, given what you've survived. And the work of seeking and finding who you really are can answer these questions and uncover the newest version of yourself. This next best version of you has been buried under piles of crap made of judgement, guilt and shame; but with unrelenting love and courage, and the support of people in your life, you found the jewel. You found your reason. You found yourself worth. You decided you were worthy of the love, energy and courage necessary to heal and become stronger and wiser than you were before the trauma. You've been stretched, pulled, shattered, crushed and polished. You're a jewel; a teacher, capable of showing all who encounter you, what is possible posttraumatically. You now, love and appreciate yourself like never before. You now shine in a way that is brilliant and irresistible. As you recover and uncover your sense of self, there is a presence about you. You radiate an energy that people around you notice, and comment on. Trauma survivors in the survivor and teacher stage of healing often hear comments like 'are you on a diet, have you lost weight, you're glowing, are you doing something different, you seem peaceful, or you look great!' What they are witnessing is the latest version of you in expression. They are witnessing the transformation from victim to survivor to teacher. They are witnessing the transformation of you into You—congratulations.

I believe that we are all here for two reasons, to teach and learn. As newborns, we teach. Clueless of the world that's really all we can do. So we do; as newborns we teach everyone around us to slow down, be patient, be loving, be trusting, be honest, be kind, be forgiving, be curious, be free. Then we grow, and we learn how to interact with others in a way that makes them feel comfortable. Unfortunately, while learning to comply and please others, we often forget who we are, and how precious we are. And we have to learn consciously, what we once knew instinctively. So the school of life goes, learn and teach; teach and learn; ideally in a loving and compassionate manner. But either way we are here to teach and learn; first ourselves, then others. The next version of you is on the other side of every experience; you get to decide if it's the next best version or not. Every person you meet, and everything you do teaches, and someone learns. Who you are, what you do, how you interact, and respond, in every situation, teaches a lesson, and someone learns. The method of the lesson being taught and learned, will depend on what stage of your journey you're on. There are three stages of being, posttraumatically—victim, survivor and teacher.

Victims are often overwhelmed by judgement, guilt and shame. They tend to feel lost, helpless and hopeless. In victim stage, constant support is needed. These people are in crisis mode most of the time, needing continuous support and encouragement. There is a reactivity in victim stage that often leaves them feeling at the mercy of their environment. There is a sense of emotional and psychological numbing and disconnection in this stage. There is little, if any sense of self in victim stage. Victims tend to say, "he, she, it, or they, made me do...say..." or "he, she, it, or they, decided to..." For victims, there is no sense of autonomy or responsibility. They draw heavily from their environment for the energy and insight needed to survive from day to day. There's almost the sense of a learning disability or learned helplessness in this stage—a fear of getting it wrong. Much like a new baby—there's a sense of fragile wonder, questioning and uncertainty. People in this stage should be supported with patience, compassion, and firm and healthy boundaries.

Survivors are often more energetic and motivated than victims. They tend to feel hopeful, frustrated, empowered, angry, motivated, impatient, anxious, excited, sad, lonely and helpful. In this stage, people are exploring their options, initiating growth and healing, participating in life's activities—socializing, support group, familial interactions. There is a sense of emotional and psychological engagement with rigid boundaries. Survivors are very protective of their privacy and space. Survivors can be both unpredictable and reliable, in their attempt to navigate social and personal relationships. Survivors probably wrestle with the issue of 'control,' more than either victims (who feel powerless and out of control) and teachers (who are coming to terms with the illusion of control). Survivors want to control everything without being controlled by anything; which is impossible. Survivors often say, "if I just do... then it'll be all right, or all I have to do is...then everything will work out, or I'll take care of it." These statements are often followed by "I wish I could but..., or sorry to cancel but..., or hey, can I have raincheck on...?" They often over work, over extend and over commit themselves and then withdraw. There is a strong need to reestablish a sense of self at this stage, and consequently, people are exploring and changing often. There's a sense of anxious learning and collaboration with the self and others in this stage—a need to get it right. Much like a child—there's a sense of endless possibility and the desire to try multiple things. People in this stage should be encouraged and supported with healthy boundaries.

Teachers are often more centered and settled than victims and survivors. They tend to feel hopeful, empowered, supported, motivated, happy and peaceful. In this stage people are making long term plans, supporting and encouraging others, taking time for personal healing and growth, exchanging ideas and plan in more spontaneous ways. Teachers tend to be more intentional and structured. There's a sense of I may not be in control of my environment, and that's ok. I am in control of how I respond to it. While this can seem rigid and inflexible to some, teachers tend to have 'scheduled spontaneity.' Teachers often say, "let's plan a work free vacation, or let's plan cell phone free party, or can I call you back when I'm not busy with work, or let's plan a road trip to nowhere..." There is a sense of emotional and psychological balance that encourages open and flexible interactions. Teachers take responsibility for how they show up but not how they are experienced. By this I mean teachers intend to present with respect and compassion for self, and others, and they take responsibility for how they present. But teachers do not take responsibility for how others choose to interpret their intent. There will always be critics. All great teachers have them; Jesus, Buddha, Gandhi, Martin Luther King Jr. Oprah Winfrey, Nelson Mandela, You and Me. We all have critics and cheerleaders. In the teacher stage, there is a difference sense of wonder. It's like that saying 'the more I learn, the more I realize I don't know. There is a sense of peace, humility and wonder around learning in this stage—a feeling of gratitude. Much like a young adult—there's a sense of competence and self-awareness that encourages and empowers the self and others. This should be encouraged and supported, with occasional reminders for the teacher to just have fun.

At any given time, anyone can be in a victim, survivor or teacher stage in response to a life circumstance. Where you are and how quickly you move from one stage to another will depend on both your internal, and external, resources. And anyone can be between stages as well; transitioning from victim to survivor, survivor to teacher, or teacher to survivor or teacher to victim. Life is constantly changing, and as stated before, you are the one constant on your journey. Your internal knowing will always call to you and guide you; with your permission. Permission in this sense means your willingness to hear your internal voice. It means following your instinct. Where you are on your healing journey—victim, survivor or teacher will affect your ability to hear, trust and follow your internal voice.

Can you identify what stage of healing you are in? Do you know if you are in victim, survivor or teacher stage? Can you identify times in your past where you were in victim stage and moved to survivor stage or survivor stage and moved to teacher, or teacher stage and moved back to victim or survivor stage?

Pause

There are lessons to teach and learn in each stage. What have you learned and what have you taught? What can you learn and what can you teach? On the following pages, you are invited to explore ways that you can share your gifts. How can you shine your light and be a source of love and support for others? This sharing of yourself doesn't have to be public or global. Sharing your self can be as small as choosing to smile and say hello to a passerby. It can be visiting a neighbor, or family member, or shelter. How you choose to share yourself and shine your light is up to you. What's important is that you do, and that it's authentic. So, think of ways that you can give of yourself, however small. Just do something consistently.

Notes

Notes

Notes

There is no wrong way, time or place to start healing. Wherever you are on your healing journey is the perfect place. That you are still alive and still trying, matters. Much like the tree on the cover, you can be doing everything right and still shit happens. That's what life is, springing forward even when it snows. The picture was taken in May of 2016. This tree sits in front of my house and inspires me regularly. It reminds me that something is always taking care of me, I call this something God/Universe. I feel like I'm living proof that there is something bigger, wiser and stronger than us working on our behalf. My 'normal' has changed so many times that either life is crazy or I am. My friends would probably say the latter. I've learned that it helps to feel what you need to feel, when you need to feel it. Be sad, mad, scared and glad when you feel it. If you don't, you betray yourself and start a series of micro-betrayals that lead to depression, anxiety and countless illnesses. These compromises invariably lead to the unleashing of your warrior self feeling the need to protect you and overcorrect. Feelings are messages that communicate how you feel about things. Don't ignore your feelings. Acknowledge them as soon as possible. If you're happy, be happy! Enjoy every second of it. Take it all in. If you're sad, be sad! Slow down. Allow the sadness to be comforted. Then get support for whatever was lost. If you're scared, be scared! Let the worry communicate its concerns without dismissing them. Then get the information you need to dissolve the fear. If you're mad, be mad! Let the anger express its sense of injustice (without harming anything or anyone). Find a way to get support in righting any wrongs. Happiness isn't about always getting what you want. Happiness is about knowing that whatever is happening right now will change, and that's ok. It about allowing change without being offended by it. Spring always comes and always turns to summer, which becomes autumn, then winter. Does it really help to complain about how much you hate a certain season? They all change! And they all come back again! This is the beautiful thing about life. It's always changing. And we are supported always; in all ways. You're still here and I celebrate your courage.

I wish you love, hope and healing posttraumatically! Be well.

REFERENCES

American Psychiatric Association. (2013). *Diagnostic and statistical manual of mental disorders* (5th ed.). Arlington, VA: American Psychiatric Publishing.

Amen, Daniel G. M.D. *Healing the Hardware Of The Soul.* The Free Press. New York, New York, 2002.

Bible Hub.com, 2017.

Child Trauma Academy. Childrauma.org, 2017.

Clark, Robin E., Judith Freeman Clark and Christine Adamec. *The Encyclopedia of Child Abuse.* 3rd Ed. New York, Facts on File, Inc., 2007.

Doctor, Ronald M. and Frank N. Shiromoto. *The A to Z of Trauma: A concise guide to the Causes, Symptoms, and Treatment of Traumatic Stress Disorders.* New York: Checkmark Books, 2010.

Handson, Rick with Richard Medius. *Buddha's Brain: The Practical Neuroscience of Happiness, Love & Wisdom.* California: New Harbinger Publishing, Inc., 2009.

Herman, Judith. M.D. *Trauma and Recovery: The Aftermath of Violence—from Domestic Abuse to Political Terror.* New York, Basic Books, 1992.

Levine, Peter A. PhD. *Healing Trauma: A Pioneering Program for Restoring the Wisdom of Your Body.* Sounds True, Inc., Boulder, CO 2005.

Rothschild, Babette. The Body Remembers: *The Psychophysiology of Trauma and Trauma Treatment.* --, W.W. Norton & Company, 2000.

Rothschild, Babette with Marjorie Rand. *Help for the Helper: The Psychophysiology of Compassion Fatigue and Vicarious Trauma.* New York: Norton, 2006.

Shapiro, F. *Eye Movement Desensitization and Reprocessing,* 2nd Ed. New York, Guilford Press, 2001.

Terr, Lenore. *Unchained Memories: True Stories of Traumatic Memories, Lost and Found.*--- New York, Basic Books. 1995.

Trauma Center. Traumacenter.org, 2017.

Van der Kolk, Bessel A., Alexander McFarlane, and Lars Weisaeth, eds. *Traumatic Stress.* New York: Guilford Press, 1996.

Warren, Muriel Prince. *From Trauma to Transformation.* Connecticut, Crown House Publishing, 2006.